Dear Sue

Thankyou for your
support
& friendship

NAVIGATE
YOUR STORM

How Regaining Self-Belief and Confidence
Brings Joy in Challenging Times

Enjoy reading!

Love
Ingrid
x

Thanks

Sawabona, "I see you".

A Zulu greeting that means I am present with you.

A few words of gratitude to all those who believed and supported me on my life journey. People come into our lives for "a reason, season, or a lifetime". Sometimes our paths will cross for an initial reason where we have common ground. This may extend to a season beyond the initial engagement, and in some cases, our relationship will extend over a lifetime. Thank you to each of you for being part of my rich and adventurous life.

Thank you to my twins, Lauren and Terrance, for their endless tolerance of my changing ideas and determination to grow and succeed. More recently, thank you to John for seamlessly making life happen in the background as I leaned into my intense desire to get this book over the line.

Thank you to Carol, Marie and Debs for your support, time and contributions to this book.

I am eternally grateful to all who have crossed my life path.

May you all live wonderful lives of joy and happiness.

Ubuntu, "I am because we are".

Contents

INGRID FEAR

Introduction

This book is for you if you feel low in confidence and disconnected.

You may have experienced a hiccup in life's flow and find it difficult to get back in. You may have lost your self-confidence and wonder where the joy in life is.

You want to feel life's flow again and require a gentle nudge and guide.

Through the vulnerable sharing of my own lived experiences, I hope to inspire and guide you. I've weathered life's challenging storms, just like you, and I believe this book can help you navigate your way forward to a more joyful and balanced life.

Water has always given me the ying and yang of stillness and energy. Thus, I have woven the analogy of a river of life throughout this book to help readers realise that we all have the power to find our flow once we have cleared any obstacles that block our way.

This easy read blends my personal story with short exercises and parables at the end of each chapter to help you navigate your way to confidence and self-belief while incorporating well-being into your daily routine.

Your story is yours to own. Remember, it is your choice to choose how you wish to navigate your future life chapters.

Thank you for your presence and time.

Please let me know how this book helps you or visit my website for downloadable worksheets to support your journey to confidence. Share this book with someone who you think may benefit from reading it.

Chapter 1

My Storm

"You can't calm the storm, so stop trying. What you can do is calm yourself. The storm will pass."
- Timber Hawkeye

Life is not linear. Always expect the unexpected. Shit happens.

"Sit down. We need to chat. I have something to tell you." These were the words I heard at the end of that day in 1998.

"I did not tell you but thought you would understand; I have signed our house over as surety to the business, which is now going bust. We will lose everything we have."

I was silent. I was wondering whether this was a joke. I had clarified this. I never trusted one of the business partners. The next few moments were blank as I entered disbelief, shock and anger. If you are familiar with the natural psychological reaction to the perceived threat of "freeze, fight, flight", and, more recently, "fawn," my initial reaction was one of freeze.

Then, I did what I did best:

Fix things.

Put on a smiley face.

Step into a role of support.

Enable and empower another so we can use this moment to do something unique with life.

I was now stepping into the response of "fight".

As a family, we had a wonderful and privileged life full of joy and happiness. We felt safe and secure and never really needed to give too much thought about spending our pennies. We lived in a fantastic climate that allowed for lazy school afternoons spent on the beach or the sports fields. My mornings were filled with ladies' tennis, socialising, and a little side hustle of tourism, where my business partner and I would take tourists for 4x4 trips into the local game parks or short journeys along the sandy beaches of the Eastern Cape in our Land Rover.

Driving on the beaches in the mid-1990s was permissible, and tourists embraced the idea that two ladies were doing what men would typically do. We often received stunned faces from male tourist clients expecting some rugged-looking men who had just stepped out of living in the bush to take them into the hinterland to view elephants and wild animals in the local national park. Their faces were even more surprised when they realised how well we navigated the Land Rover Defender through the rough terrain and sandy beaches. We were two very confident and capable ladies with much self-belief and daily embracing of life. Every day resulted in belly laughing. We were happy with our lot. Life was simple, fun and family-focused.

This side venture fitted in very well around family life, so I could enjoy regular time in nature allowing me enough time to get home, cook dinner, have a glass of wine, and make sure one of us read to the children who were in bed early and ready for school the next day. A tongue-in-cheek phrase is often used in Africa when everything is calm, and life is good, "Life in Africa is tough." Little did I know what was about to hit me and what "tough" meant.

Our future was unclear. Overnight, we went from bright dreams, plans and laughter to stress, constant tears, humiliation, embarrassment, anger and a lack of clarity.

For those aware of Maslow's hierarchy of needs, a motivational theory is often presented as a pyramid and states that humans are motivated to fulfil their needs in a hierarchical order. This order will begin on the lower rung of the triangle, where our most basic needs of food, water, warmth, rest and shelter must be met before we seek out more in life, such as a better job. Our motivation at this level is derived from our instinct to survive.

We found ourselves on the lower rung, seeking water, food, warmth and shelter, which we needed to survive.

Maslow's theory states that the ultimate goal is to reach the pinnacle of the triangle, where we are in a space of self-actualisation. In other words, when we seek to achieve our full potential without needing external motivation. This is likely to be very different for each of us.

As a family, we had yet to reach our full potential, the fifth level, but possibly level three, where we sought to continue to develop our love, friendships and sense of belonging within the community and remain connected to family and extended family.

Due to this situation, thoughts ran through our heads, "Where are we going to live? How will we feed ourselves?" Our income had just dried up, and everything we owned was no longer ours, as the bank would repossess what it could. How do we tell our friends and family of our situation?

It was a moment of unexpected choice and a pivotal moment in life. Life had just changed unexpectedly. We had not seen the storm brewing. We were unprepared and did not know how to navigate forward.

We both needed jobs to earn enough money to eat, have warmth and shelter, and be secure. My little side venture of off-road tourism would never provide the shelter or food we had become accustomed to. Thoughts about the impact on our twins, who were eight years old at the time, included, "We must not let the children's lives change."

After a few weeks of walking around in a daze and disbelief while constantly considering all options that might be available to us to be able to survive and hopefully begin to climb back up the ladder to where life would be much easier and far more fun, we opted for an extreme choice.

We decided that we would leave the country and begin again in another country, moving into the "flight" response. To this day, I am unclear whether this decision was driven by our need to survive or our belief that "it was not possible" to continue to survive and grow in South Africa due to our situation.

We needed to flee the storm and remove ourselves from an environment where this situation had badly dented our egos and hurt our pride or sense of self-respect and self-esteem. Indeed, my confidence was knocked as I churned over how I could have avoided this situation. I stepped into blame mode, not responsibility.

This extreme choice meant we would move to the United Kingdom "lock, stock and barrel." After all, I had a British passport, and the United Kingdom offered incredible IT work opportunities just ahead of the then-dreaded Y2K bug, otherwise known as the Millennium Bug. It was a time when the world was anxious about what might happen when the clocks ticked over at midnight on 31 December 1999 to the year 2000. In the 1960s, engineers used a two-digit code for the year, leaving out the 19. As the year 2000 drew closer, computer engineers wondered whether the systems would interpret the switch from "19" in the date to that of "00".

The world's anxiety did not match our anxiety about our uncertain future.

We packed our lives into boxes within six weeks of the initial bombshell message, storing everything and selling the furniture we could not keep. We knew that whatever home we could find in the UK would never be able to accommodate the volume or size of furniture we had in South Africa. We had to strip ourselves back to the bare minimum and keep things simple. We made callous decisions. I have a robust family value, and much of our "stuff" had emotive attachments to my past and that of my grand and great-grandparents.

My husband had secured a job in the UK, and they wanted him to start immediately. The idea of him starting within the next few weeks appeared promising, but I was not ready to leave the country. He flew out to begin his job in an unfamiliar country and work out where we were to live so he could easily commute to this new job. The kindness of amazing friends who offered him accommodation during this "discovery phase" reduced any additional significant costs. We remain eternally grateful for this and have subsequently "paid this forward" over time. I believe in paying forward kindness, which does not always have to go back to the person who instigated the kindness. Keep the energy of kindness moving and flowing.

I refused to leave the country until two things happened, and both were important to me. I now understand that these were my values playing out.

Firstly, I wanted to attend my youngest brother's wedding in Cape Town, where I would have an opportunity to say goodbye to my immediate and extended family members. This wedding was due in the upcoming weeks. With meagre finances, I had yet to determine if we could ever afford to return to South Africa. This thought of lack of possibility and disbelief in future opportunities was not typical for me. I was so low in confidence and self-belief that I told myself this would be the last time I would ever see my close and extended family again.

We borrowed £5,000 from my dad to hold in our account so that the UK would accept us as not a liability to the system. I wanted to repay this loan before seeking a permanent home in the United Kingdom. I was having consistent thoughts like this, even though the pressure had not come from my father. My value system was playing out again, driving me to do the right thing. Dad was not bothered and was being kind (It took me three years to pay this back in small chunks). Ironically, I used the image of a triangle with building blocks in the triangle. Each block equated to a value of £50. : I would colour in one block as I paid back each £50 enabling me to see progress in my goal.

Secondly, I had set up a temporary home in a small two-bedroomed house on the outskirts of town to keep the children in school and maintain some normality until the wedding. This would be a natural end to their school term, and their next school chapter would start somewhere new in the UK. It felt like the right thing to do for the children and me. So, within storms come storms. And while we were in the storm of major change in our lives, I had not considered the impact of a Bailiff knocking on my door, announcing he had come to collect the car as part of the collateral for the business that had folded.

This was my breaking point. This life storm had just become real and there was nowhere to shelter.

Everything I had ever owned – our house, cars, boat, dogs – and life, as I knew it, had been taken away, not to mention my pride, self-belief, confidence and joy.

I know others have been through some tough times in life that may be far more serious, and although this was not my first life storm, this one felt different. It had stripped me of being me. My first life storm was losing my mother a few years earlier after a lengthy battle with bone cancer. The loss of your best friend at a time when your twin children were eighteen months old was incredibly emotional and confusing. I was not sure how I was meant to feel. It was a release for her from all her pain, yet the saddest moment in my life, realising that a loving, kind and fun granny was going to be deprived of time with her first grandchildren. They would be deprived of never having the pleasure of her endless love and kindness.

This loss, this storm of life, was different. I had not expected this of life. I had put my trust into the partnership and assumed life would go "tickety boo" and assumed that my role in life was quite simply to raise the children and dabble in hobby jobs (as my mother had done). I was repeating the family system's beliefs and possibly the culture's beliefs at the time. A man provides, and a woman supports.

Well, this supporting act was not rewarding me as I had expected.

After crying many tears and drinking all the remaining wine in the cupboards (after all, we could not ship the wine stock to the UK), I headed to my brother's wedding in Cape Town on a national bus with the children. This turned out to be yet another embarrassing moment as close friends came to wave their goodbyes at the bus terminal. Usually, I would have flown or driven to Cape Town. We were not used to using public transport to get to another destination in the country. The new financial situation disallowed this opportunity.

The wedding was beautiful and, selfishly, an incredible opportunity to see family as we said our tearful goodbyes for now or forever.

One final farewell still had to happen at the airport before we headed to the UK. This farewell was to my dad, one of my most supportive people in life. While we never really talked about the reality of the situation, he knew exactly what was going on. He had loaned us the £5,000 in good faith to support our next steps, enabling us to enter the United Kingdom without burdening the benefit system. Little did I know how much this loan of £5,000 would be one of my turning points in life. The embarrassment and shame that we could not fund our way to new pastures ate at me. It became my mission to pay every penny back as soon as possible so we could begin our lives again.

The memory of that goodbye is as vivid today as it was that day. I held back my tears to stay strong for my dad and the children. I was unsuccessful. The floodgates opened, and I recall doing one final look back over my shoulder as we turned the corner into the security area and the unknown of our future.

INGRID FEAR

Chapter 2

Choice

"I am not what happened to me. I am what I choose to become."

- Carl Jung

While I did not fully grasp the meaning of this powerful quote, I was beginning to work out that life throws curve balls just when you think all is going well. Various situations may steer you from your plan, assuming you have one. I was also beginning to think that maybe I could be more than I believed. I needed clarification on what needed to happen or what my next steps might be. I needed to deal with what was in front of me.

Change.

It was change in every way possible: new life, new country, different weather, people speaking with new accents and new currency. Given the exchange rate, it all felt costly. Our first trip to the grocery shop in the UK felt like it financially crippled us. We were all in shock and the children's pocket money was twenty pence per week. Yet we accepted, in the main, that this change would be an exciting opportunity.

Yes, I had lost my self-belief, and yes, I carried anger, and yes, I was sad.

Despite this, I had to be there for the children. I had to help them integrate into this new life that we had led them towards. Anyway, I like an adventure, and if I reframed this next chapter of my life, I could treat it as an adventure. We could travel to Europe and explore cities and countries that were otherwise difficult to reach from South Africa. I am always the eternal optimist.

Simple things like understanding the school system and working out logistics about the geographical location of the schools relative to where we were staying became a real focus. Previously, it would not have mattered as I would have jumped into a car with the children and driven them to their new school. Now, without a car and without money to buy a car, we relied upon public transport, which is incredible compared to South Africa's public transport availability. Not having our independent mode of transport to get around was new ground for us and a steep learning curve. Another drain on my confidence, was the lack of ability to be independent.

Silly me, I wrongly assumed that the first school we approached would have space for the children. Nope, we had to go to the next village, which meant a five kilometre bus ride or walk in one direction. "Everything for a reason," as the saying goes. What an excellent start for the children and us as a family unit, as the people we met through the new school became the foundation for our future social life and ultimately led to a sense of community and belonging.

Some families we met at this school remain part of our lives over 25 years later. I am eternally grateful for their kindness and lack of judgment of our situation. The way they offered their homes and time to support the children, allowing them time and opportunity to transition into the world of the UK, gave hope and began to bring laughter back into our lives.

There were days when the pennies did not stretch far enough for me to afford a bus return ticket home after dropping the children at school. Instead of feeling sorry for myself, I would walk the five kilometres back from the school, often in driving rain and blustery wind. I reframed my thoughts about the return walk to be good for my health. I had yet to learn about the power of a mindset reframe. The return walk gave me time to reflect upon my situation.

Within a few weeks, we had made the windowless bathroom and two-bedroomed rented flat our home. We settled down into a routine of going to work and school. We even found ourselves getting pet gerbils to give the children some normality.

The gerbils gave hours of entertainment as they redesigned the sawdust tunnels in their fish tank home. It was less exhilarating entertainment when they escaped their home and shredded the floor-draped curtains of the rented flat.

We had some light relief in the flow of life as we met new people and enjoyed our new, safe environment. There was a lot of learning to "flip thoughts" to keep ourselves upbeat. Learning to reframe or "flip the thought" from hostile and upset to noticing the positives and opportunities around us became a family game. Instead of saying, "It's raining again," we would say, "How lucky are we to walk in the rain without worrying about the safety of our lives?" Instead of thinking, "We don't have enough money for a car," we would say, "Look how fit we are getting from all this walking." Instead of lamenting how we missed our friends, we would focus on the opportunity to make new friends.

Reframing is a beautiful way of shifting the mindset from focusing on the negative to possibility, opportunity and optimism. "Flip the thought" was a game we played regularly, and soon, we noticed that life was feeling brighter. We were tricking our minds into seeing a better way forward.

This simple reframing helped us move through the change curve quickly. I had gone through all the elements of the change curve, from initial shock to denial (going to the wedding before leaving the country). Anger had set in, and I oscillated between the change curve stages of "anger" and "experiment". I experimented with living in a new country with an open mind while meeting new people.

At the end of this chapter, I will share how you can reframe your thoughts to help you feel more optimistic. Before I do this, I would like to explain how we think. Here comes a very light science exercise.

Our minds are influential! It is where thought happens. Everything in life begins with a thought. Thoughts result in our actions and behaviours. We have something like 70 000 to 80 000 thoughts daily, depending on what book you choose to research this information. Wow, all those thoughts each day? No wonder we are exhausted at the end of each day. Of course, we are not necessarily conscious of every single thought that passes through.

The challenge is that being human, our natural default in thought errs towards negative thoughts and those of fear. We have had to focus on the negative to survive as a species over millennia. We have had to seek out the danger and threat to our lives, so we constantly unconsciously seek out what does not work, what is wrong, and where the threat is. We seek out the potential problems that could get in our way of success. Hence, we have a negative thought process. A shift in thought process is required to learn how to grow and handle change better in modern times. Learning to become more consciously aware of our thoughts so that we may direct and choose how we move forward is empowering.

This is challenging – simply navigating our day-to-day lives and activities in a modern-day world where we have to make decisions with a brain system that remains wired to help us survive and flee from danger.

We are complex creatures. Our brain is advanced enough to allow us to develop in science and technology. Yet, it still holds onto some primitive features, including the limbic system, the oldest part of our brain.

Bear with me, as this section could be complicated. Yet it is valuable to be made aware of some basic functionality of our brains.

Simply put, today we only need to be aware of two parts of our brain: the back and the front. The "back brain" is correctly known as the limbic system, and the "front brain" is known as the prefrontal cortex.

The limbic system helps us sense when we are potentially under threat or when danger may be upon us, making us anxious. It operates at speed and is dominated by emotion and impulse. While it is responsible for our essential survival functions such as breathing, heart rate and body temperature, because of its speed of response to situations, it can let us down in a modern-day world as we react with behaviours such as aggression or dominance. Clearly, these are unacceptable behaviours or responses in society today and will result in having a negative impact on our wellbeing and social acceptance.

A few helpful tips to notice whether you are allowing your limbic system to run the show more than it needs to in modern-day life are if you often live in a state of fear or anxiety. Or perhaps you are unwilling to be open to new thoughts and find yourself relatively rigid in your thinking.

It's time to learn how to tap into the front brain more often.

The prefrontal cortex is our most recently developed part. It operates more slowly and is what we use to think more rationally and logically. I like to call this the CEO part of our brain. It is where we make significant decisions after processing and rationalising all the information. It is less reactive, and this slower rationalising process can be helpful to us as we reframe the situation, which leads to improved confidence and self-belief.

Learning to consciously shift my thinking from the reactive limbic system into the more rational prefrontal cortex was valuable. It has helped me overcome challenges as they arise, and it is also helpful in reducing emotions such as anxiety or fear.

I spent a lot of time understanding how to develop a new way of thinking that would leave me inspired and energised at the end of each day instead of drained and depleted. I had noticed that being constantly reactive and using my back brain meant that I was always angry and blurted out my thoughts, which sometimes became a little embarrassing.

The more I practiced slowing my thoughts, the more relaxed I felt and in control of each situation.

The more I practiced this, the easier it became. I guess you could say I developed a new habit, for which I am grateful. This new pattern of thought resulted in a more optimistic view of life, which naturally contributed to rebuilding my self-belief and confidence.

You see, we are not conscious of all our thoughts each day, yet each thought creates an emotion that ultimately results in an action we will take. This happens at such speed, and sometimes, our reactions surprise us a bit. For example, I resigned from a reception job in the heat of the moment after being disrespected by a local squash club member.

This was one of three jobs I juggled to help us regain financial stability. I had previously played squash to a decent level, but now I could not afford to play it and would instead work at the reception desk as I watched people bounce into the squash club to have fun.

I found myself in a situation where a member came to the desk without greeting me or looking at me while talking to someone else. He demanded I change his booking from one court to another because he did not like the court allocated to him. He spoke in a tone that made me feel disrespected, hurt, angry and not seen for who I was. I was livid and incensed. My reaction was to stand up, walk around the desk so I was square with him, hand the pen over to him, and say, "I am not your servant. I am another human being who happens to be able to play squash better than you." I picked up my bag and left the building and the job.

Only once I got home did I begin to process what had happened and how embarrassed I was about my unnecessary reaction. I have no idea of the actual thoughts I had at that moment, but I am confident they are not printable in this book. The point is, while I was unaware of my actual thoughts, I was very aware of my emotion and behaviour.

Had I known that I have the power to choose a new thought that would result in better emotion and behaviour, I may still have had the job!

Thoughts trigger emotions that result in action.

I could have had a completely different outcome had I chosen to hit the pause button on my recurring thoughts of anger against this member and instead select a kind thought like "he clearly had a bad day." This alone would have reduced my angst and stress at the moment. The great thing is, as you will hear me repeatedly say throughout this book and in life, you have a choice. You have a choice in every single moment to create something new and different, particularly if you do not like the outcome of your behaviour or the feeling you become aware of.

Some things are in our control, and others are out of our control. I was not in control of how he addressed me that day, but I was, unknowingly, in control of my thoughts, feelings and reactions. We are not able to change the situation. The situation is the situation. It is what it is. Accept the situation. What is within my power and where I get to make a choice is how I could react to the situation. Phew! Powerful stuff.

We all can choose how we think about any situation or storm that crosses our path. That in itself is a choice.

I regularly practice this and share it with almost all of my coaching clients when they tell me their situation is "hopeless".

A more likely result in being happier can come from slowing down the process of our reactive thoughts, stepping into using the prefrontal cortex to rationalise, consciously becoming aware of the thoughts we possibly have, and then choosing a new thought that is more compassionate and kinder to ourselves.

As one of my favourite authors, Viktor Frankl, wrote in his book, 'Man's Search for Meaning', "Everything can be taken from a man but one thing: the last of the human freedoms, to choose one's attitude in any given set of circumstances, to choose one's way."

Each day, we get to choose how we wish to show up and what attitude we want towards a person, the day, work and life in general.

How do you choose to move through life? Are you open-minded about all things new? Are you curious about exploring new ways to have fun or find joy in life? Or are you choosing to stay as you are while you judge others for giving life a go?

Remember, you do not have control over another person's thoughts. It is within your gift to choose how you respond to their actions and behaviours towards you.

We all have life storms and many different thoughts. Some of our storms may appear small to others who have endured and weathered many intense life storms. Yet, when we are amid our respective life storms, big or small, it can sometimes feel overwhelming and exhausting. Like swimming upstream against the current.

My storms include dealing with the death of loved ones, three redundancies, and, of course, the storm I have just mentioned, one of debt at an age when I thought life would move in the direction I dreamed of. And a storm that was yet to come is that of divorce. All of these storms result in change. Each storm was a situation that was outside of my control. At first, I had not realised that I had the power of choice of thought to help navigate my way through the storms.

The point is that life is a constant flow of stormy waters; sometimes, it is a torrential downpour that denies us time to shelter and find safety to navigate our way out of the stormy waters. And sometimes, in these stormy waters, if unbalanced and lacking self-belief or direction, we end up sinking or swimming upstream, which becomes exhausting.

Learning to find a way to anchor ourselves and step into sheltered or calmer waters so that we may gather our chaotic thoughts, rationalise, and see the storm for what it is rather than catastrophize the situation can help us calm ourselves down. We can reframe our thoughts to direct ourselves into a more helpful emotive state that enables us to move forward with choice rather than be blown in the direction of the wind.

Storytime
Adapting to the Flow

An older person slipped on a wet rock near the edge of a river and fell in. As onlookers watched in horror, the person was swept towards a high waterfall.

There was great joy when they emerged bruised but unharmed further downstream. "How did you survive?" asked someone as the crowd gathered around. The older person responded, "Instead of trying to make the water accommodate me, I accommodated myself to it. Instead of fighting it, I relaxed into the swirl, allowing it to shape me. I worked with the force of the water instead of against it. That is how I survived."

Exercise
Be Your Own Best Friend

I have demonstrated this reframing exercise throughout the above chapter, and you will continue to see it throughout this book. I believe this is one of the most useful, powerful, yet easy-to-do exercises. It raises your self-awareness about your own negative thoughts.

Perhaps the next time you notice yourself putting pressure on yourself by saying something like "I must/should go to the gym." Stop and think about the pressure you are putting yourself under. Words such as "must" and "should" add unnecessary pressure to us. I wonder if you notice how often you might say these words.

Sometimes, the reframe is as simple as giving yourself permission to do nothing and "just be." Taking time out of life to notice how you feel and what you might be thinking is compassionate and kind.

The "Be your own best friend" reframing technique is perfect for helping you shift your mindset to a new perspective and a more positive and joyful outcome. You may even find that you have more confidence and joy in life!

How to be your own best friend.

1. Accept your thoughts are just thoughts.

2. Notice the language you are using in your thoughts.

3. Ask yourself, whether your thoughts are kind.

4. Question yourself whether you would say these thoughts out loud to your best friend. If the answer is "no", continue onto step 5.

5. Become curious whether your thought language adds or reduces pressure on you.

6. Write down your thoughts. Example: "I must go to the gym to do my exercise even though it is a lovely day outside today."

7. Reframe the thought by rephrasing it to be kinder or optimistic. Example: "It's a beautiful day. I will exercise in the fresh air today with a walk instead of going to the gym."

8. Read the new reframed thought out loud with zest. Own it.

9. Notice how you feel after saying the new reframed thought out loud.

10. Repeat this process each time you catch yourself being unkind to yourself in thought.

Practicing reframing your thoughts, statements, or responses into more helpful, kind, and optimistic responses will help you rewire and reprogramme your neural pathways, resulting in a happier and more confident you.

Today is perfect for beginning a happier and healthier way of thinking. Be patient and kind to yourself. The choice is yours.

Reflections

A space to capture your thoughts and ideas.

Chapter 3

Reflection

"Knowing yourself is the beginning of all wisdom."
Aristotle

What do I want now?

What needs to change?

How do I move forward?

There are so many tough questions! Sometimes, I found it easier to speak the answers out loud so I could hear my thoughts.

I learned to face my fears, mainly as I realised what I wanted and needed to change. I had to believe in myself, find courage, and be confident enough to take bold steps to create a new life that would (hopefully) bring me joy again.

Self-reflection reminded me that I was to blame for finding myself in this life situation of wanting change. No one else was to blame for how I was feeling. It also reminded me that I had grown. I learned that I needed to be kinder to myself and not keep putting myself down. I needed to put myself first for a change. After all, I had made some bold and courageous decisions for a better future for all. The intent had always been positive. I had lost myself in this process.

As a family, we survived the ordeal of moving countries, integrating into a new culture, and growing as individuals.

We had become very resilient, and our eyes had been opened to new possibilities in the world. We had become optimistic about what lay ahead. We had overcome many obstacles.

We stretched our comfort zones together, found new friends, and began settling into a routine again.

Financially, we were beginning to find our feet and breathe, allowing space to pause and self-reflect. We had achieved our goal of owning a house again and having a small financial nest egg helping us feel more secure.

It was me who wanted more. I wanted to do something meaningful. I had grown in confidence over the last few years. To survive and keep moving forward, I had been on autopilot. I was so determined to get through and not fail. The cost of this was my energy, and I had lost focus on what was important: happiness.

I know that happiness is a state and is not found through the purchase of luxury items or events. Happiness comes from within and loving yourself. Through my journey of self-growth, I had discovered the profession of coaching. The coaching journey culminated with my life experience, which helped me reflect on beliefs I had of myself and the world that held me back from achieving internal happiness. I learned to create new beliefs and adjust my value system to help me move forward to a new future.

I believed I had to do it myself if I wanted what I was dreaming of. I had begun to think I could no longer rely on another to help me get what or where I wanted. I had to do this myself. I did not want to be disappointed by another or to let another down. Independence became one of my biggest drivers.

Another part of my self-reflection journey was visiting my personal values in life. Understanding these values helped me move forward.

It is always good to know your values so that you can remain true to yourself. Learning to know when to flex my values became a lesson of mine. The fierce protection of my value of "independence" would sometimes get in my way of accepting help and support.

I went through these reflection questions over and over again.

Who had I been? A strong, confident, outgoing, carefree, healthy, happy mother who was full of love and trust. Someone who had assumed she was infallible and life would provide without effort.

Who am I now? The obvious is the mother and wife and all the labels that go with life. And with these labels, I realised I did not like the person I had become. This person deserved more. This person deserved to find happiness and gain the self-belief she once had. This person was no longer the same.

What do I want now? A new life, health, happiness, financial independence, personal growth, fulfillment, adventure, the ability to travel the world to see family, options, choice.

I wanted to be able to choose, to be in control of myself, and to help and support others in living lives of choice, happiness, and confidence.

What needs to change? Three things.

1. Mindset

2. Supportive tribe

3. Ongoing personal growth

These three shifts would give me the key ingredients to move me towards my new future.

Mindset is key. An optimistic, open, and self-believing mindset will help you achieve your new goals. A winning formula is having your mind work with you rather than against you. To accomplish this optimistic, high-performing mindset, I needed to adjust how I communicated with myself and my language when speaking with others.

Self-reflection highlighted that how I spoke to myself and of myself to others needed to switch from blame and judgment to being more supportive, encouraging, and optimistic.

The language that I and others around me used was limited, such as "it's not possible," "I can't," "it is too hard," and "it is too expensive."

My dialogue needed to change. Choosing new ways to communicate had become an obsession, and I am now quick to pick this up when coaching my clients.

"Shut the duck up" became a mantra of mine. Whenever I heard myself saying "must, should, cannot," my duck mantra came into play.

Supporting tribe. I had people around me who left me feeling depleted and drained, people who took my energy and sapped me completely. I call them mood hoovers. If you only ever take one action to improve your life and make it more joyful, it is as simple as hitting the "delete" button on the mood hoovers in your life.

You know those people who only reach out to tell you their problems, dump on you, and then leave without so much as a question about how you might feel yourself? These are the same people who are not around for you when you need help.

This filtering of tribe members included deleting people who projected their limiting beliefs onto my dreams and aspirations. A limiting belief is a belief that gets in the way of you achieving something or doing something differently. I was surrounded by unsupportive people who said, "You will never make it; life is tough, and you have to work hard to get what you want." These were their limiting beliefs about me and my capabilities.

People who had given up in life. People who refused to grow. People who lived their lives through the lives of magazines, news, and media or work colleagues, thus not facing their world. People who judged. People who were not prepared to try new things in life. Phew, quite a cull of people was required. Of course, this did not happen overnight; in some cases, it took a long time as I slowly extracted myself from these social environments.

Ongoing personal growth. To achieve what I dreamed of, I would need to learn more about myself and the ways of others. Growth of self was paramount. I needed a meaningful purpose to keep me motivated to steer my way forward. Stagnation was not an option. Having grown up in Africa, I know what stagnant water does. It kills you! So, finding a way to flow into cleaner and calmer waters was what I needed to learn. Anyway, learning more about how we as humans function and how we underestimate ourselves was beginning to get very interesting, exciting, and energising.

How do I move forward?

Make the changes within me. Stop blaming and begin to carve out some baby steps to move from dream to reality. Set up small goals that will lead to the big goal of financial independence and a sense of freedom while living a meaningful, balanced life of wellbeing and contribution to others.

Action required stepping out of the pool of reflection and returning to the flow of the river of life. I would need to change course to get into a flow of ease in this river of life. I was not required to flow where the river took me as if I were a piece of driftwood; I needed to directly carve out a new pathway and build in strength at a pace that worked for me.

I knew this would take more work, and I was aware that more obstacles may be in the way, interrupting my flow.

In summary, whether you are facing or withstanding a storm in your life, find time to regularly self-reflect on what serves you well and what no longer serves you well. Reflection time is excellent for personal growth, mental wellbeing, and self-confidence. Knowing what you stand for. Acknowledging your successes and reflecting on areas you want to change or tweak is empowering.

Observing behaviours and reactions to events and situations in the day enables you to do things differently, think different thoughts, and take other actions. Equally, reflection time gives you an understanding of what you wish to have more of in your life.

I recommend carving out regular self-reflection time into your day, week, or month to help you increase your self-awareness. This will enable you to manage your future better. Self-reflection also allows you to live your life in alignment with your core values, leading to making the right decisions for you more often.

A word of caution when self-reflecting is to be mindful that this activity may activate your inner critic; genuine self-reflection comes from a place of neutrality and non-judgment, simple observation. No judgment, just notice.

Imagine feeling in control and confident with your decisions, actions, and behaviours in each situation.

Storytime
The People on the Other Side of the River

One day, a person visiting a faraway land came down the hill from the village they had been visiting. They had enjoyed their time in the village, where the people were kind, fun, and interesting. Approaching the riverbanks, they met a ferryman.

The person asked the ferryman to take her across the river to the village on the other side.

Once on the ferry, she asked the ferryman, "What are the people like on the other side of the river?" She had heard from others that the people on the other side of the river were unkind, boring, and sad.

The ferryman responded to her and asked how she had found the people in the village that she had recently visited.

"I found them kind, fun, and interesting."

As he rowed the little boat across the river to the next village, the ferryman said to the person, "Then, I think you will find the people in this village to be the same. Kind, fun and interesting."

Exercise
Reflection

If you want to try self-reflection and make it a regular practice, here is a little exercise to help you kick-start it.

Several ways exist to self-reflect, and they generally include journalling, meditating, and being curious about your life activities over time. You may be curious about yourself and the areas you want to develop or improve, such as a better career, improved health, a different attitude, or increased self-awareness.

- Begin by finding a quiet space where you feel comfortable and will not be disturbed for a few minutes.

- Decide on the activity you will use to reflect, e.g. journal, meditate, or engage in more active reflection, which may include going for a gentle walk.

- Raise curiosity by asking yourself open questions such as, "Is what I am doing making me happy?" "What am I grateful for?" "Is how I talk to myself kind?" You may also choose to use the questions I used on myself mentioned above in this chapter.

- Ask yourself these questions and pause to "hear" your responses.

- Notice your thoughts and responses with no judgment. Trust your gut and intuition during this moment of curiosity.

- Journal or write down these responsive thoughts, enabling you to reflect later, as you continue your curiosity and increased self-awareness.

- Notice your emotions.

- Schedule this time regularly so you can observe the pattern of thoughts.

- Choose to act or to sit with your new awareness.

- Enjoy raising your self-awareness and getting to know you better.

Reflections

A space to capture your thoughts and ideas

INGRID FEAR

Chapter 4

Changing Course

"Yesterday, I was clever, and I wanted to change the world. Today, I am wise, so I am changing myself."

- Rumi

In nature, rivers change course over time due to rocks, obstacles, or debris that block their flow. As the river becomes increasingly blocked, it begins carving out a new course.

Nature knows how to survive and keep momentum. It keeps adapting to the barriers and obstacles in front of it. Nature also knows that to survive, it needs to be able to keep itself fuelled and watered. A tree knows when to lie dormant and restore its energy. Equally, the tree knows when it is time to push new boundaries, reach for sunlight, and stand tall.

I had learned to tune into nature, observe how it adapted, and kept returning to life after each storm; whether the storm was intense heat, a deluge of rain, or long periods of freezing, it had a way of never giving up. Nature had become my companion and healer, where I felt connected and calm. It remains my daily source of fuel. Having noticed how nature can reach the sunlight and stand tall, I decided to do the same to find my natural flow again. A new course of life needed to be carved out.

How do you carve out a new course in life?

It sounded straightforward until I started thinking about what this meant. It would require some tough decisions and discussions, letting people down, digging deep to stay on course, energized, and finding courage within myself.

Having spent much time self-reflecting and becoming self-aware was empowering, and I no longer feared change. I learned a lot about myself, how I behaved, what I believed, and what I liked and disliked. I learned that you cannot hide from yourself. Knowing who you are, what you want, and how you handle certain situations gives you energy and confidence.

Not fearing change was a significant shift for me. Change was something to embrace. Change, of course, is constant. The sooner we learn to accept that change will happen whether we like it or not, the easier it becomes to navigate.

Some changes are outside of our control, so there is no value in getting upset about what we cannot control. The one thing that we are absolutely in control of, particularly in a time of change, is our thoughts. It is within our gift and power to choose our thoughts about any situation.

My turning point was understanding the power to choose our thoughts and ways of life. The power and energy I felt, realising that despite the storms I had faced thus far in my life, it did not have to be this way. I could choose to navigate my way through the storms thrown at me in life.

I was at a choice point in life where I was consciously choosing how to navigate out of the storm and into calmer waters. The choice I was making to navigate forward was to change course dramatically.

Sadly, one of the life decisions I made that impacted many people close to me was that of choosing to get divorced. This was a major shock to many around us, but for me, too much had changed; too much water had flowed under the bridge. I was tired and my perspective on this situation was that I had shifted into a new path in life. As a partnership we were no longer heading in the same direction. We were in separate boats, moving at different speeds in the same river of life. There was tension in our directions. We had a conflict in our navigation skills and wanted a different crew on our journey.

It was very important to both of us that this was amicable. While the word "divorce" sends shock waves to families and communities, this decision was mutual, and no one was to blame. Life had played a few cards; we had responded in our own way but were left exhausted, and neither wanted to travel the other's way.

I do not want to underplay this significant moment in life. The confusing emotions of loneliness, freedom, shame, guilt, sadness, and anxiety were constantly interchanging within me. Unfortunately, I could not shake away the fact that trust had been broken. I knew that the intention was always positive. However, as I've learned, your reaction to life events will result in an outcome. The outcome is not always one that you anticipate or hope to achieve. For me, the triggering event was signing our house over as surety to the business without my consent or knowledge. The reaction was anger and moving countries. The outcome was a loss of trust and a feeling of disrespect. A sense of inequality.

Even though this decision caused unhappiness to our children and wider family members, deep down, I knew it was a good decision for me. I was learning to stand up for myself and make essential choices for myself and those who depended upon me.

At this choice point in life, when I was ready to take back my control and step into the helm to navigate a new course, life threw a few additional storms at me.

I had already been made redundant twice and the third occurrence was about to play out. Yet the strange thing is that making such a clear decision to change course and knowing what and how I wanted to move forward made navigating the other storms more manageable.

During this time of changing course, I was also spending a lot of time with my uncle in Scotland, who was battling several illnesses, including pancreatic cancer. Not having a partner or children of his own, and me being the only blood relative in the UK with him, it was my honour to be a part of this stage of his life. Strangely enough, it was a very therapeutic time for us both as we shared our innermost thoughts and worries and supported each other in this challenging time.

Many years previously—amongst the vast variety of self-development books I had read, also known as "shelf development ", if you choose not to read the purchased books—I had read the book titled, 'The Secret' by Rhonda Byrne. This book drew me and many others in. It was the first time I had encountered something called the law of attraction. This law of attraction is a philosophy that positive thoughts will bring positivity. In contrast, negative thoughts will bring negativity into your life.

The law of attraction is based on quantum physics: Like attracts like. The energy we attract depends on what we emit. Imagine that the mind is like a magnet, radiating and receiving frequencies to and from the universe. Each thought we have sends out a signal, which gathers similar frequencies.

This made sense to me. My recent thought pattern had been one of negativity. I was attracting a constant barrage of obstacles and challenges into my life. It was like swimming against the tide. There was undoubtedly no ease or flow in my life.

To support changing course, I also required a new thought pattern; a new way of thinking and a healthier mindset that defaulted to optimism rather than negativity. I wanted to create an opportunity to attract more of the right energy and people into my world. Some would say it was time to change the channel and tune into a new frequency. A frequency that would open me up to new people and environments who operated on the same wavelength.

I needed to switch to a different frequency to help attract what I wanted. Thus far, I have changed course by making the tough decision to change my marital status. I have learned to reflect and shift my mindset to one of optimism. I have become aware of the power of language and how to be kind to myself in thought. I have also recognised that I needed to change my vibration to a frequency that supported where I was heading.

During this period of growth, I also learned the power of visualisation. Visualisation is nothing new to anyone; we do this every day when we imagine what our day will be like. Perhaps we imagine what items must go on the shopping list or maybe we dream about the evening after work.

Visualisation is used to assist people in several ways. It is proven to contribute to improved performance by sportspeople and help people achieve the desired success. By holding an image of what you want to achieve or be, you allow the subconscious mind to direct you toward your goals. Visualisation can be a powerful tool for shaping your subconscious mind. I will return to the subconscious mind later, first, I want to share a story with you about the power of visualisation.

One of the most powerful visualisation stories I have ever encountered was that of William Trubridge, a New Zealand world champion and world record-holding freediver who, in 2013, became the first freediver to dive deeper than 100 meters. To practice free diving, apart from the obvious physical and equipment preparation, William used visualisation. Imagining the temperature of the water, the depth of his dive, the pressure on his lungs and the movement of the ocean while he held onto his breath and practiced his breathing techniques was how he had been able to mentally prepare for the sport of free diving.

A lovely quote to support this practice is: "Visualisation is daydreaming with purpose."

Let's get back to discussing the subconscious mind. It acts as a data bank of thought patterns that drive your behaviour. By visualising positive outcomes and engaging your various senses, you can learn to re-programme your subconscious mind. Aligning your subconscious mind to work with your consciously chosen goals can lead to beautiful outcomes.

Note that I mention visualising positive outcomes! I know that we often visualise adverse outcomes and then wonder why on earth we get the results we get. Let me explain. You know the saying, "Be careful what you wish for." Think about it: how often do you wish or hope that something does not happen, and it happens?

For example, you think, "I don't want to spill this tea on the new white carpet." And what happens? You spill the tea on the new white carpet. You see, the subconscious mind does not "hear" negative language such as "don't". Instead, it hears the instruction to "spill the tea on the white carpet".

Try this out now. Don't think about a pink elephant.

What happened? Have you just visualised a pink elephant? Bet you did! My point is that what you think about, you create. So, begin to think about what you do want.

The subconscious mind refers to the parts of your brain that you're not fully aware of but hold thoughts, feelings and ideas that influence your conscious mind and subsequent actions. It's a very confusing part of the brain, as you are unaware of how much it affects your behaviour. Trying to understand it can be quite a challenge. I know that it works. And if people like William Trubridge or your top sports people in the world are tuning into visualisation and the subconscious mind, then it has to be a good thing.

When you begin to grasp the subconscious concept, you can use that part of your brain to overcome struggles you are consciously aware of. Just remember that it can affect you negatively and positively! You choose how you wish to use it.

As I was carving out this new course in my life, I began visualising consciously what I wanted, committing these images to my subconscious mind by looking at the visual images each day. I had pictures around my desk and walls at home that kept reminding me of what I was focusing on.

I still do this today. You step into my office, and I have images on the walls and in my goal-setting files.

Be mindful of your internal language and how you are subliminally instructing your mind on what to focus on. We go about our day unconsciously, thinking about life, the day, work and what needs to happen next. As we think these thoughts, we subliminally instruct the unconscious mind. We are not always conscious of all of our thoughts.

I like to pause daily and give myself a little "check from the neck up" on my thought pattern. A perfect time to do this is when you notice things are going awry. Stop and think about what you have just been thinking about. What kind of language have you been using? Was it positive, or was it negative?

You will agree with me by now that it is important to think positively and use encouraging, kind, and supportive language to help build confidence and inner self-belief.

To gain more confidence requires a shift in your self-belief. You can help yourself with this right now. One way to do this is to think well of yourself. You can build your self-worth by becoming mindful of how you feed yourself with thought. Each time you think ill of yourself or your dreams, counter the thought with something positive or an idea of possibility. Also, make sure that you "keep it real". Sometimes, we think about an upcoming event, project all sorts of concerns and worry about the possibilities of what might go wrong. None of this is real! You are creating something that may never happen; worse, you are investing so much of your energy in making this concern a reality. Instead, invest energy into thinking about how well the event can play out. Remember, worry is negative goal setting.

We must learn to re-wire our thought patterns to be kind and helpful.

If we are always thinking about what we do not want—"I do not want to fail"—the dominant thought is on failure, not success. Instead, visualise the success we wish to achieve or the progress we want. Thinking thoughts such as, "I am confident and worthy of this new role,"; "I am happy in my relationship,"; or "I am fit and healthy and love walking in nature" are going to send out a different vibration to the thought about failure. And, of course, we will naturally be drawn to and attract activities that lead towards success rather than the outcome of failure.

Initially, the ability to relax my mind through the imagery of walking along a beautiful long beach on a warm summer evening gave me such an incredible feeling of calmness. I noticed that I could be creative and dream of a future different from the one I was bumbling into.

I also learned that visualisation is super powerful if you tap into all your senses by imagining the colours, sights, sounds and smells you might experience in the imagery. It is also a much more powerful way of setting a goal than the boring way of scribbling a few sentences in black ink on a white piece of paper. It is so much fun to dream the image, draw the image and pop the drawing up on the wall for you to see each day.

Do you want to know what I visualised and how I changed my course? I found time to myself and sat in nature near some running water. I had paper and a pen, and I began taking a few deep breaths to calm and centre myself. I played some guided meditation music that focused on dreaming about the future.

Before the meditation, I focused on one question: "What do I want now?" I let this question "go" as I eased into the meditation. Once the guided meditation music had been completed, I continued to sit silently and hold onto the images I had visualised.

Next, I opened my eyes, picked up my pen and paper and began capturing what I had visualised in keywords and images. I kept scribing until the image had faded. Remember, these images will disappear if you do not capture them immediately.

This is very powerful, accessing what the subconscious mind shares with us. As you may have worked out, the subconscious mind speaks in pictures and images, not in words. You only need to think about any dream, and you have to know that it is true. I bet your dreams are in pictures and not in words.

So, what did I visualise? How was I to change course?

I visualised a confident, self-believing, happy person who was excited about life and who continued to grow while supporting others. I visualised being able to step into my power of being me. That "me" was happy, healthy, confident and surrounded by family and supporting friends. This person lived in a happy home filled with love and laughter and had a little stream running by. This visualisation also had me empowering others and being on top of the world. That image remains vivid today because I have become this and live in a happy home filled with love and laughter with a stream running by!

The next step was to look back to the law of attraction and take action. It is all well and good vibrating on a level that moves you towards your desires and dreams, but I believe we must help ourselves, too. My next step was to take practical action, deciding to bring this image to reality.

One decision was absolute for me: continue to develop myself. I believed that continuing to grow and learn would create more opportunities for me while widening my network and helping me find my tribe. Growing myself would improve my confidence and help me understand who I was. I believed this would also help me find more joy. I needed to step away from data-driven IT environments that completely drained me and move more towards a people-focused world.

I shifted into developing people through leadership training and coaching.

My confidence grew stronger as I continued to work on myself through self-development training and reading. I looked within and knew exactly what I stood for. I explored my personal value system and began unpacking my purpose in life. The latter took some time. Once I had discovered this, there was no stopping me. I was completely energised and noticed the shifts in how I stepped into each day: excited, energised, clear and confident.

Finding your reason for being, or your "Ikigai", as they say in Japan, is exciting and energising and keeps you on point daily.

I believed in myself. I thought that I could bring my visualisation to reality. Others around me did not. I hit the delete button on them. I wanted to surround myself with people who topped me up and not depleted me. I wanted the cheerleaders, not the mood hoovers.

To summarise: changing course in your life requires courage, clarity, effort and action. As with anything, having the right attitude or mindset to support your changes and enable you to see new possibilities is essential.

Stepping out of your comfort zone, having the courage to make tough decisions and stepping into the unknown and less safe stretch zone is where the growth happens.

It's essential to ensure you have the right like-minded, optimistic tribe support team around you, enabling you to drive forward. Move away from those who drain or deplete you; perhaps these people disbelieve in your dream.

Learn to visualise where you want to go or what you wish to have so that you can work as one unit with your subconscious mind. This will help guide and support you on your new course in life.

Be clear about what you want and take action!

Storytime
The frog that never gave up

This is one of my favourite stories. I could not leave it out of this book. Enjoy!

Once, a bunch of tiny frogs arranged a climbing competition. The goal was to reach the top of a very high tower. A large crowd gathered around the building to see the race and cheer on the contestants.

The race began.

No one in the crowd believed the tiny frogs would reach the top of the tower. Heard throughout the race were statements from the crowd such as:

"Oh, that is way too difficult."

"They will never make it to the top."

"Not a chance they will succeed."

"The tower is far too high for little frogs."

"They will all fall."

"It is an impossible task!"

Sure enough, the tiny frogs began collapsing, one by one, except for those who, in a fresh burst of energy, were climbing higher and higher. The crowd continued to shout that it was too difficult and that the frogs would never make it to the top. As each moment passed, more tiny frogs got tired and gave up.

The little frogs could hear the crowd and most believed that they were probably right.

One little frog continued to climb higher and higher. This one refused to give up!

The crowd continued to berate and smirk at him. This frog would not give up. Towards the end of the race, all had given up climbing the tower except for the one tiny frog who, after a considerable effort, was the only one who reached the top! All the other tiny frogs wanted to know how this one frog managed to do it. They wondered how the little frog had found the strength to reach the top.

They learned that the winning frog was deaf. He had not heard any of the crowd's negative comments and disbelief in their ability to climb the tower.

Remember to be careful who you listen to and what you listen to in life. Do not sabotage yourself, your life or your dreams.

Exercise
Visualisation

As a reminder, visualisation is imagining what you want to achieve in the future as if it were an actual event today. It works best when you involve all of your five senses: sight, touch, taste, hearing and smell. This process will direct your subconscious to be aware of the goal you have in mind.

Visualisation is a powerful tool that can be used to help build your confidence and self-worth. It is like a mental rehearsal for the reality you wish to create. It can be used for various life events, such as imagining how you will deliver a presentation that lies ahead of you by imagining the environment, the audience and, more importantly, how you wish to be and feel while presenting. It is helpful to mentally immerse yourself fully into this presentation space.

I know someone who loves rosemary. To help with the consistency of a powerful image of visualising her confidence when presenting, she pops a sprig of the herb on her lapel or in her pocket both during the visualisation exercise and in the reality of presenting.

Similar to self-reflection in the previous chapter, this will require you to find some space where you will not be interrupted. As an aside note, self-reflection is about reviewing the past to improve your future. Visualisation is imagining how things could be better or different, so the beginning stages of designing a new future.

Below are the steps that I follow to visualise what I wish to achieve.

- Create some quiet time and a calm environment to visualise.

- Know what you want to focus on.

- Close your eyes if it is comfortable and safe.

- Take a few deep breaths to calm down and connect with yourself.

- Begin to cast your thoughts at a specific time in the future.

- Imagine yourself being or doing what you desire to achieve.

- Picture yourself in your imagined image. Notice all the sights, sounds, colours, smells, temperatures, tastes and feelings around you in this image.

- Embrace all the wonders of this image as you inhale deeply.

- Hold onto all those fantastic emotions, feelings and images for as long as you can with your eyes still closed. Be there.

- When you think you have absorbed as much as you can of your image and are ready, gently open your eyes. Come back to the here and now. Open your journal and jot down keywords to help capture what you saw, felt and heard. Draw the images you have just imagined so that you capture the image in its entirety, including all the senses you were aware of.

And, yes, you can draw. There is no judgment on your drawing. It is simply another way to capture your imagined image and will help you reconnect with this image on a deeper level. Have fun.

- Post this image on a wall near your laptop or in your car, somewhere that you can see each day, to help further reimprint it into your mind. Perhaps it is a screensaver? Thus, allow the subconscious mind to work with you to steer you toward your visualisation dream.

Enjoy the process and your growth. Notice how you begin to believe in what you can achieve. I look forward to hearing how you get along with this exercise.

Reflections

A space to capture your thoughts and ideas

INGRID FEAR

Chapter 5

Clearing the Deadwood

"Get rid of clutter, and you may find it was blocking the door you've been looking for."

- Karina Mayer

"Don't tell anyone else. We plan to climb Kilimanjaro, and we only want positive people. Would you like to join us?"

Oh, my goodness, what an exciting offer that was when I needed some excitement. Having made the tough decision to divorce, it had given me the headspace to consider what was next for me. I was becoming clear about what I wanted: adventure and challenge were high on my list. I thought it would be a stretch if I had an adventure and leaned into an unknown and uncomfortable space. Expanding my comfort zone would result in my personal growth because of the coaching training I had participated in. I would raise my self-awareness and find more confidence because I had stretched into an area that would be new for me and involve new and different people.

Reaching the summit of Africa's highest mountain—also known as the Rooftop of Africa—would be a new and challenging experience requiring a lot of training. Climbing to a height of 5895 meters would be challenging and was unknown territory for me.

One of my motivations was to explore more of Africa and feel the "beat of Africa" again. For those of you who know, once you have the feel of Africa in your blood, it is tough to ignore the magnetism to head back to that fantastic continent of vibrant energy and stark contrasts, with diverse people who get on with life.

I knew one person who wanted to take on the challenge of climbing Kilimanjaro, so I called him immediately to let him know about the opportunity, and he said, "Yes," without hesitation.

I was beginning to learn that the answer to almost anything was "yes" unless it crossed my values and beliefs or would harm me. It was such fun to say "yes" to invites and opportunities offered. What an excellent way to embrace the new and discover different environments and people. Strangely enough, the more I said, "Yes," the more exciting things came my way.

And so, having agreed to climb Kilimanjaro, I went walking. I walked to work and back. We walked in the evenings and at the weekends. We climbed Snowdon three times over a weekend as practice. Time on legs, they said, keep walking. The days on Kilimanjaro would be long and slow in pace, so we had to train to be able to walk on different terrain for eight hours a day.

Walking involves talking, eating, laughing, crying, community and well-being. It was therapeutic and good for my soul and my fitness. This period of six months leading up to October 2012 was pivotal in my life. I met amazing people. I learned to love walking to the point that I still walk on any holiday I go on. It is a beautiful way of getting to know the country and environment. Through walking, I got closer to nature, which energised me every time.

When you are walking for hours on end amongst nature, you begin to notice the sounds and smells around you. I started to get curious about the different bird songs. I was curious to identify the bird song with the respective bird. This curiosity and interest remain with me to this day. I discovered plants such as wild garlic and thistles. The funniest name for a wild plant was "sticky willy". If you pull this plant away from another plant, it sticks to you and is quite prickly, hence its hilarious name. I learned new things every time I stepped out the door in my walking boots.

I had a focus. I was clear about what I was doing and why I was doing it. I was in my stretch zone, stepping into a completely unknown zone. I had no idea whether I could summit, but I decided to give it my best shot.

I was energised by having something new in the diary. Something that people dreamed of doing but never acted upon. I visualised getting to the summit of the Roof of Africa in all sorts of weather. I read books and articles to understand more about our conditions as a team. The exciting thing was that whatever article I read or whoever I spoke to who had already experienced this climb spoke positively of it and said it was a "must do" in life. They believed in me being able to do it. It was the people who played safe around me that were doubtful. "It is too high," they said. "You will have to sleep in a tent for seven nights." "It will be sub-zero temperatures." "What if the people that go with you are weird?" "What if you don't make it?" "It is expensive." "Too many injections." The neigh sayers were looming and waiting for me to fail.

I focused on the messages that said I would love it, which was a privilege to experience. My children were beyond excited for me and were a huge encouragement. Together with my dad, they were my biggest cheerleaders at the time.

I began believing that I would make it. I knew I would make it. I was certainly not doing all this prep work and traveling all that way without seeing whatever it was to see on the top of this mountain that rose above the clouds of Africa.

As a forming team, we bonded solidly. We grew to know each other inside out. We encouraged each other and removed doubt from one another. Positive people only. No mood hoovers. Bliss. Healthy people. I realised who my tribe needed to include, outdoors-focused, positive attitude, adventurous, life is for living. People who had balance. No extreme thoughts or judgments. People who wanted to grow and support. People who spoke with optimism and pace. People who were accountable for their being and who did not seek to blame life, politics, family, and work for their current outcome in life. People who focused on possibility and health. People who carved out time for themselves and did not sell their souls to work or moaned that life was boring. Oh, and this new tribe also enjoyed a glass of wine or two to keep the balance.

As with any new activity in life, you need to find time. Our calendars are full. Most of us need to earn pennies to put food on the table. We have families and life commitments. I learned that you can find time and space to make something happen if you truly want something.

Desire and self-belief are what is required to get ahead in life.

I had to let go of some things to create this time in my calendar. I had to clear any "dead wood" that was in my way and blocking my progress.

One thing that I could not let go of, and was very high on my values list, was my regular trips up to Scotland to visit my uncle. He was beginning to go through a bit of a rough patch with his pancreatic cancer. As his only blood relative, we became very close and shared many stories of courage. He had been the brave family member who had chosen to leave our country of South Africa at a time when he felt restrained and judged by society. He found the courage to find a place in the world that supported him, embraced who he was and allowed him to be himself without judgment.

While training to climb Kilimanjaro, my twins were carving out their lives in the wider world. One had joined the army and would be on tour in Afghanistan when we climbed Kilimanjaro. The other twin had chosen to research sharks in the Bahamas and would send me photos of her diving with Tiger Sharks! My parental nerves were constantly being challenged. I had taught the children to be independent and grab life with both hands. They were doing just this, so "if you can't beat them, join them" was my approach.

Let's climb this mountain!

I had a focus and was clear about the prep that needed to happen. But what about the deadwood that needed to be cleared?

To get back into the flow of life and have the energy I had all those years before leaving South Africa, I still needed to pay attention to a few things holding me back.

While I had self-reflected, learned about being kind to myself in thought and words, visualised what I wanted and believed in myself, there was still work to do. I had to clear the way forward for an easy run and flow to my destination effortlessly.

Some of this deadwood was internal and some was tangible or external to my being. Clearing physical deadwood is easy. It is like weeding the garden; weeding the mind of the internal deadwood would be more challenging.

Why is it important to clear the deadwood even when energised and focused on this amazing new adventure? Well, having a clear pathway makes it easier to move forward. Removing obstacles or unloading the unnecessary from your backpack, so to speak, will make for a lighter weight on your back and, therefore, a more straightforward journey forward.

I decided to begin with the easy stuff, the physical deadwood. It was as if spring had arrived in my life for the first time in a long time.

I flung all the cupboard doors open, whether in the kitchen, bedrooms, garage, or loft and began clearing the clutter or deadwood.

I was soon on first-name terms with the people at the tip and the local charity shops. They were so grateful. One person's clutter is another's treasure. The act of clearing your clutter is very therapeutic and energising.

Clearing the physical clutter lifts your spirits. It creates physical space around you, relieving you of feeling "bogged down." Sifting through a pile of your clothes to find the one shirt you want to wear is irritating, time-wasting and unnecessary. If you no longer wear clothing items, release them from your space. Stop holding onto them and let those who need those items benefit.

Giving things away to charity brings a sense of joy. The act of giving is a great way to improve your own well-being and overall mood. Clearing the cupboards created a sense of relief as I began to act and get back in control of my physical space.

Old tins of paint in the garage? Gone. I would buy fresh paint and paint the walls a new colour. Why be bound by the colour stashed in the garage for a few years? It felt powerful to make this decision. Anyway, I needed space for walking poles and walking boots.

Next, I created time in my calendar to go walking and training. This was relatively easy, as I had noticed that many of my activities supported the desire to be fit and healthy for climbing Kilimanjaro. I ditched a few social activities that I deemed unnecessary and unsupportive of my current focus.

House decluttered, the physical space felt uplifting and light. The calendar had been cleared of the unnecessary items and space for training had been made.

Next, the tough one. Decluttering my mind of any remaining deadwood that would get in the way of me moving forward and holding onto this incredible energy I was experiencing meant clearing any emotional clutter.

I had already learned to reframe and was very aware of the importance of optimistic thinking and the value of a mindset that supports excellent performance. I wanted to explore two things further to ensure I had a supportive and enabling mindset. These two things included visiting my habits and any limiting beliefs I may still hold. If I were to clear the deadwood, it would be best to clear any internal deadwood, too.

Before discussing habits, I want to point out that it is an absolute fallacy to think you can create a new habit in 21 days. There is a lot more to habits than most people realise.

Habits are initially created by us to help with efficiency and reduce the volume of conscious thinking as we perform specific tasks. Imagine if we had to think about our every move as we go about brushing our teeth or making a cup of tea. Both are habits that we have created along the way. We know that we are brushing our teeth or making a cup of tea, but we are unaware of every step of the process. We perform them without real thought.

Some habits are worth holding onto, and others need a little upgrade or rewiring to align with the life that we are now living. For example, waking up in the morning and turning on the news on TV first thing could be a habit. This habit will, by default, fill your head with images of problems and issues worldwide. A rewire or an upgrade of this habit could be waking up in the morning and listening to a podcast by Deepak Chopra or meditative music on Spotify, filling your head with calmness and thought-provoking information instead of issues and problems that you are often outside of your control anyway.

People love to get involved in other people's stories and what is outside their control. Focus on your own life and what is within your control. Fill your mind with the right messages and information instead of stacking up more deadwood, which can make you feel heavy, stressed and anxious about what might be.

Perhaps you noticed actions or behaviours that no longer served you during your reflection exercise. If so, some of these may be habits that require being part of the clearing of your deadwood process. A few things need to be in place to create a new habit. Firstly, there must be a desire to want something new and different. Next, you must feel that you are being rewarded for the new behaviour.

Of course, creating a habit requires a repetitive routine to help rewire the neural pathways. Your old habit may be overridden but in a time of stress, depending on how ingrained the old habit is, you may revert to the old habit.

Let me explain through the analogy of using a grass field to help people understand what it takes to create a new habit. This will require you to use your imagination. Imagine there is a field of long grass that you need to walk through each day on your way to school or work. You go through the same "kissing gate" daily to enter the field. You walk the same path daily to the exit "kissing gate" on the other side of the field. You will walk this route twice per day, once each way.

On the first day, you walk in this field of long grass where there is yet to be a path. You will notice that the grass behind you springs back up. One day, after having trodden this path twice per day for a lengthy period, you see that there is no longer grass in the path and only a well-trodden sand path, making it easy to identify your route without thinking about your next step.

We liken this pathway you created to a neural pathway in your mind. This well-trodden neural pathway is, in fact, your thought process, where you have made a path or a pattern of thought. Let's call this the new habit.

This is precisely how you will do this daily until you decide you want a new pathway. Then, you must perform the same exercise and carve out a new habit or neural pathway.

Creating this new pathway may take longer or less time, depending on the frequency and desire you have within you to create a new path. I hope this makes sense to you. The habits I chose to rewire were easy changes for me, and it took only a short time before they became my new way of doing things.

The first was that instead of switching on the TV in the morning to listen to the news or any other unhelpful stories being shared, I listened to a carefully selected ten-minute YouTube burst of inspiration and learning. This was before the delights of the many beautiful podcasts we can choose from today.

Next was a simple switch: I no longer bought and read trashy magazines to entertain myself in my moments of boredom. Instead, I invested in and began reading self-development books on topics I was curious about.

Another habit I changed was walking to work twice a week instead of driving as part of my training. The desire was strong, and the reward was that it contributed to my walking training that week while creating more time in my calendar for different activities over the weekend. I must admit that once I had summited Kilimanjaro, this healthy habit was no longer part of my weekly routine. The desire had changed in intensity.

My next focus to help mental decluttering was exploring limiting belief systems I might have held. Belief systems run deep within us. We have beliefs that support and hold us back, referred to as limiting beliefs.

Before moving on, I want to ensure we are all on the same page to understand a belief. A belief is something that we have created along our journey in life. As we go through life, we make meanings from the world around us. Those interpretations and perceptions are recorded by the subconscious mind and then become the beliefs or rules by which we live, often without us being aware that we are doing this. The challenge is that when we carry these beliefs into our adult lives, they are no longer helpful to the lives we now live.

Something as simple as being told as a child that you had to eat everything on your plate, or you would never grow up to be big and strong. As a result, you ate all your food, whether you were hungry or not. As an adult, you continue to do this because you believe you must eat all the food on your plate, whatever the volume, so that you can remain big and strong. This belief must consider whether you need all the calories on this plate or whether the food is nutritious.

Beliefs are not facts. Beliefs are based solely on our generalisations from our experiences in life or other people's messages about us and the meaning we make from this information. Many people I coach often come to me believing they are unworthy of success or unable to change careers. They hold these beliefs within themselves because of what they have heard. Messages and instructions were shared with them when they were children. Perhaps someone—often in authority—said, "You cannot spell properly. What hope have you got of ever being successful?" Or "Just find a steady job and stick with it." "Don't complain! Just be grateful for something you can do and earn money."

The sad thing is that we don't consciously decide what we believe. This means many unhelpful, limiting beliefs are stuck in our brains.

I want to give you an example of my limiting belief, which still plays havoc with me when under pressure. My limiting belief is that I cannot do maths. Where does this come from? While at school many years ago, I was told by a teacher who disliked me—because I joined her literature class late in the academic year—that I was a "maths dropout" and would "fail at literature, too".

This comment was made a few times, and it stung me. Each time I heard that comment I began to doubt my ability to do maths ever again. It was true that I had dropped out of maths classes in favour of studying literature. I had evidence and proof of what she was saying to me. As she was the teacher and an authority figure, I began to believe her. I am indeed a maths dropout, and the result is that I would never be able to perform any tasks involving maths. That meant many of the careers I was targeting were now off my list. I believed that I was probably not clever enough to go to university.

A flippant generalisation comment can influence another person's belief system and how they live their lives.

I am happy to report that what she said of me is rubbish!

I can do maths when not under pressure and aced literature without this teacher's help. In fact, I am writing this book! If I held onto this limiting belief and deemed it true, it would have prevented me from having a fantastic career of coaching, training, and facilitating others to be terrific people and leaders.

Returning to the task at hand: summiting Kilimanjaro. I needed to shift my belief that I would not summit and would be the one to hold everyone back on the mountain.

Instead of focusing on the messages that fed the belief that I would hold people back from summiting the mountain, I began to reflect on messages and stories that had been told in my youth that were more helpful and supportive. This enabled me to shift my belief into "of course, I will summit".

These were phrases that I had often heard from my dad, who would say things like:

"You can do anything you want in life. Do it well. Enjoy what you do. Be humble and have respect for others."

I had seen my dad study in his forties to get a better job and promotion so that we could have a better life. I had seen him respect others. I had seen him enjoying all that he did, and, in my eyes, he did everything well. He believed in himself; he had confidence in himself and his children. He believed in my brothers and me, and he had told us to go into the world and make it ours.

Simply by reminding me of this faith and belief that one of my biggest cheerleaders had in me, I could "shut the duck up" of the schoolteacher I had previously allowed to have power over me and my thought process.

I imagined I had a quacking duck on my shoulder, and each time I heard Mrs. X putting me down, I would sweep my hand over my shoulder and say, "Shut the duck up. I've got this and will prove to you that I am worthy and will be successful in summiting the mountain."

Clearing the deadwood left me feeling more powerful, confident and vital to continue this new course. I was stepping into being me again. I had found a new tribe of adventurers and held onto those people who I knew were solid and would support me.

An excellent relationship quote is, "People come into your life for a reason, a season or a lifetime." I found this helpful when deciding who needed to stay and who needed to be put on hold without feeling guilty about shifting the relationships. I am sure many who stayed will be part of my life forever.

I was growing and stepping out of my comfort zone. Life energised me and my thinking process was positive and supportive.

I was clear about who I was now. I was clear about what I wanted now. I had carved out a way forward.

The mountain was my first step towards the new me. It enabled me to focus on something new. After summiting Kilimanjaro, I focused on other changes I wanted to make in life. I felt back in control of myself—one thing at a time.

Nothing could stop me.

On 19th October 2012, twenty-five of us set off from Heathrow for our eight-hour flight to Nairobi. Once we landed in Nairobi, it would be another short one-hour flight to Kilimanjaro. Our climbing adventure had begun.

There was a feeling of excitement and trepidation on the flight. There was no going back. Only when you fly from Nairobi to Kilimanjaro in a tiny thirty-seater plane do you realise just how high Kilimanjaro is. Our flight flew below the summit of the mountain. We would be climbing higher than we were currently flying in a plane. Ouch.

The Kilimanjaro route would cover one-hundred kilometres over six days at altitude, the latter of which would be a new and daunting experience. Again, we laughed, cried, ate, drank water, sang, slept, drank ginger tea, and ate sloppy porridge.

I remember belly laughing one night in the food tent as we discussed the day and felt the joy and freedom of not having a care in the world. All we needed to do each day was make sure we had enough water, food, and clothes—

and put one foot in front of the other until it was time to stop, eat and sleep again. What absolute bliss! What freedom. Far away from the expectations of others and a world of technology and pressure. Instead, we were in nature in thin air with a beautiful, supportive group.

The summit was challenging, and it felt like it took forever. On summit night, we started at 11.30pm to head towards Stella Point for sunrise. One foot in front of the other. Freezing temperatures. The ground was solid and hard. We snaked up the mountain with our head torches showing the way. I found it difficult to distinguish between the row of head torches and stars. This confused me and distorted my perception of how much further we still had to go before reaching the summit. There were dancing lights everywhere on the mountain. We seemed to be in the darkness of the night for a long time. My water pipe froze, so I stopped drinking water.

We would take a few steps forward and then pause as we gasped for air at the high altitude of five-thousand meters. My calves were screaming at me because of the intensity of the gradient of walking uphill. Words of encouragement rippled through the now twenty-three people on our team. Unfortunately, two people were hit by altitude sickness and it was deemed too dangerous for them to continue going up to the summit.

One thing no one ever tells you about Kilimanjaro is how you lose all inhibitions in an attempt to conserve your much-needed energy. At the lower levels of the mountain, if you needed to have a bush wee, you would walk a few meters away from the team and do what was necessary, as nature called. The higher you go, the less you care about what others think and more about what energy you need to get yourself to the top.

Sneaking off for a nature call became less of an event and far more accepting that this was natural. We would take a few steps away to conserve our energy and the team would look the other way. Back in line, we would all move forward together. I was in awe of our guides' strength and positive attitude, who would summit regularly as part of their job. They gave up so much to support us in getting to the top.

On summit night, my backpack became too much for me. It was getting heavy, and I was feeling lightheaded. Just like unpacking unnecessary stuff from your life backpack (in this case to get myself to the top) I had to let go of the whole backpack! I had no energy left, and the bag was too heavy, causing me to overheat even though we were in subzero temperatures. If memory serves me right, we summited at minus six degrees. We had started our journey up the mountain in the lower humid tropical foothills of twenty degrees a few days previously.

And then, suddenly, daybreak.

I will always remember the image of the earth's curvature as dawn broke. We paused to breathe in this image. The red horizon of the earth. This was curved and not a sunrise that we had witnessed before. You could literally see the curvature of the earth. This was different from a sunrise I had seen in Africa or the hills of Surrey in the UK. Tears welled in our eyes at this moment's pure beauty and stillness. None of us had ever seen something so beautiful in our lives. At its best, nature reminds us exactly how small we are yet supports us by bringing us light, warmth, and energy at the right moment.

As the sun rose, its warmth thawed the water pipe to my camel pack water storage so I could drink again. The sun also warmed the ground we were walking on, making walking more difficult as our footsteps sank into the sandy track. We kept moving forward slowly.

And hours later, we heard people singing and congratulating us! We had made it! We threw our arms in the air and wished each other congratulations.

Our leader, Joel, said, "You are not there yet. This is only Stella Point. If you want to make the final journey, you have another hour before reaching Uhuru Peak." Gutted! It was like having run the marathon, completed it, and now being told you have still run a further ten kilometers when you have "nothing left in the tank". We were depleted of our energy and our willpower.

We chose to take a breather and regroup our thoughts and ourselves. We refuelled on the snacks we had left. We were exhausted...and each of us had to work hard on our inner dialogue to get ourselves into the right state to continue this journey as we realized it was, in fact, a further two hours of walking at a high altitude! One hour to Uhuru Peak and another back, and then we still had to get back down the mountain to our tents, which we had left at 11.30pm the previous night. It was now about 8am or 9am the next day. We had been on our feet for at least nine hours at altitudes between four and five thousand meters.

Breathing time was over, and we had to keep going to make our way to Uhuru and leave enough time to get back down the mountain to our last base camp.

We found our positions in yet another snake-like line as we returned to our mantra of "pole, pole" a Swahili translation for "slowly, slowly" continuing our steps toward Uhuru Peak. We were digging deep. Each step felt hard. No air. It was tough. Our fuses were short with each other. One person stepped out of line to capture the glacier we were walking past, which meant we all had to stop. Someone shouted, "Get back in line; it is only an f****** glacier!" It demonstrated how short our fuses were. Our tolerance for anything but reaching Uhuru was very low.

And then, there it was! Uhuru Peak with its well-photographed sign proving that we have reached it. We looked around and congratulated each other as we burst into tears again. We had made it. It was done. We took the obligatory photographs and, within ten minutes, turned and slowly returned to Stella Point.

Once we got back to Stella Point, it was a free-for-all. We no longer needed to walk slowly; we could increase our pace as we descended the mountain. We were no longer required to worry about altitude sickness. The lower we went, the easier it would become. Our focus was to get off the mountain as fast as possible so we could breathe easily again.

Suddenly, there was no team. It was almost each person to themselves. I was out of there on my own, sliding off the mountain as quickly as I could. I had practically run down that mountain, sinking into the sand with big steps. I needed water and rest. It was about sixteen hours since we had started the walk to the summit further down the mountain. It was a very long day filled with many mixed emotions.

The elation happened the next night once we had reached our final camp, where we could have showers, sleep in beds, eat pizza and drink a few beers! The relief that we had made it to the summit of Kilimanjaro, was immense. The camaraderie amongst us will never be forgotten. The self-belief, confidence and joy that I felt was one to bottle and take forward into my life.

I had overcome challenges that few would ever experience and, in doing so, had literally and figuratively "left my shit" on the mountain. I had come down from Kilimanjaro summit renewed, energised and believing in myself.

I learned that we can achieve anything if we set our minds to it, if we have the right attitude, mindset, people around us and determination to succeed. As Viktor

Frankl says, "Whatever the mind can conceive and believe, it can achieve." I also learned that life is, in fact, quite simple. As humans we overcomplicate things in our need to be accepted, liked and approved when, in fact, all that is needed in life is community, communication, love, fellowship, warmth, sleep, food and water.

Kilimanjaro was my high in 2012. I was invincible! "Bring it on," I said.

Life has a habit of grounding us. Just when I thought all was well, I had found myself, regained my confidence and found joy in my heart again, life threw another curveball.

This time, I was stronger and could handle things better. This storm had not been on my radar. I did not see it coming and it would take all my new habits and renewed energy to navigate through it.

Before moving into that unpredicted life storm, a short summary of this chapter. Clearing the deadwood requires visiting your life's physical and mental areas. Find the courage to make the necessary changes to live your best life of confidence and joy.

Remember, habits are formed for a reason at the time but may not always serve you well as you make changes in your life. Challenge your belief systems, as they may be holding you back.

Learn to say "Yes" to new things and stretch your comfort zone.

Storytime
The clouds are running

Recently, a young adult looked out from the train's window and shouted, "Dad, look, the trees are going behind us!" As his dad smiled, a young couple sitting nearby looked at the young adult's childish behaviour with pity when suddenly, again, the child exclaimed.

"Dad! Look! The clouds are running with us!"

The couple couldn't resist and asked the father, "Why don't you take your son to see a doctor?" The father smiled and said, "I did. We are on our way home from the hospital. My son was blind from birth, and, today, he sees with his eyes for the first time."

Never judge another for you do not know their full situation.

Exercise
F*** it Bucket

Who you are is what you believe. What you believe determines what you do, your choices and how you do them. This practical and straightforward exercise will help clear the deadwood without too much thought.

Create a rubbish bin by using something like a small empty flowerpot. I call this a "F*** it Bucket". Anything that no longer serves you can be thrown into the bucket and walked away from by following the steps below.

- Write down the name of the person or thing you believe is in your way of moving forward.

- Scrunch up the piece of paper.

- Physically throw the paper into the F*** it Bucket.

- Tip the contents into the household bin.

- Inhale deeply and let out a loud and long exhale.

- Repeat the breathing exercise a few times.

- Walk away from the bin with no further thought.

- Observe your feelings, thoughts, and actions after this simple act.

- Turn your focus to something new and exciting.

This exercise can be performed visually too if more helpful in the moment.

To work on clearing any belief systems you think are holding you back, I suggest you work with a coach, or someone trained to work with beliefs. It may be more complex for you than I am proposing.

Reflections

A space to capture your thoughts and ideas

INGRID FEAR

Chapter 6

Whirlpool

"No one saves us but ourselves. No one can, and no one may. We ourselves must walk the path."

- Buddha

"There has been an accident. Your dad was in the accident, and he did not make it. I am sorry." These words rang out on the phone as I picked up a call from my cousin in South Africa on 21st December, 2012.

Summiting Kilimanjaro in October 2012 brought joy, confidence, self-belief and excitement into my world. It had been a very long year, filled with sadness and challenges. My extended family had already "suffered" suicide during the year. It was a year that would rock my world and impact my future in a way I could never have imagined.

I was exhausted and emotionally drained. Work had been demanding and my boss at the time, who was to be one of my most influential cheerleaders in life, invited me to a last-minute lunch to wrap up the year and put it behind us. We need to remind ourselves of the successes we have had and shift the focus from pressure into one of acknowledgment and celebration.

We sat in our favourite pub in Weybridge, where we occasionally meet. My bag was on the floor near my feet. Inside my bag was my mobile phone. I had chosen to be present with the lunch to hand and ignore the world around me for the next two hours. We did this successfully as I ignored the constant vibration of my mobile phone in my bag.

I was so tired of constant calls back to the family in South Africa, providing them with updates on my end-of-life uncle in Scotland. I had taken it upon myself to be the connector, the communicator and the commuter up and down the country to ensure he had the care and the company he required. I took it upon myself to have those deep and challenging conversations about death that too many people avoid.

It was only five days ago that I was sitting by my uncle's bed in a hospice, reading to him the letters and recollections from family members about the impact he had on their lives. I thought it was better to do this in life than in the afterlife. This resulted in lots of giggles, tears and warmth of love.

On this Sunday, before I left Neal for the week in hospice care, he said he had one final wish: to be able to see his brothers one more time. This was a challenging request as both brothers resided in South Africa while he was in hospice in Scotland. I promised to extend his wish to his brothers and reminded him that it was the end of the year and flights might not be available.

I spoke with my uncle's brothers that Monday evening to convey his wish. Being one of the brothers, my dad surprised me and said he would consider it and discuss it with the travel agent the following day. Lunch ended with many good wishes for the upcoming Christmas, and we promised to see each other in the new year.

I looked at my phone to see who had been trying to contact me so many times. My cousin, Lindz, is also based in South Africa. My initial thoughts were irritation of me not even being able to grab a Friday Christmas lunch out and away from the constant reporting back to the family on the health of our uncle.

I arrived home and called my cousin to update her on the status of my uncle that day. I was met with a frank tone and her angst as she instructed me to "stop talking and listen". Surprised by this tone, I did exactly that and was met with the following words.

"There has been an accident. Your dad was in the accident, and he did not make it. I am sorry."

Disbelief and shock.

How was this possible? Dad was due to arrive in the UK in two days, and the plan was that we would rush up to Scotland to carry out his dying brother's wish of seeing each other one more time. And now, Dad had beaten his brother to the finishing line of life. Before I knew it, I was arranging two funerals in two different countries within days of each other.

It is said that things come in threes. A week after returning from Dad's funeral, my divorce papers were served on me. Excellent timing.

This was the final D in my 3D storm: debt, death and divorce.

My storms are no different from your life storms; only the content and people involved in the storm differ. The great news is that, as humans, we can bounce back or, better still, bounce forward stronger.

I had learned to accept that change was part of growth and each storm in life, whether small or large, gave me more experience and tools to continue to grow stronger and stronger. I had a healthy dose of resilience.

People talk about being resilient as being able to "bounce back" to where you were before being hit by life's challenges. Well, it cannot possibly be true that you bounce back to where you were. I understand the concept. Having navigated your way through your storm of life, you are more likely to be in a stronger form than you were before life's challenge.

Each knock we have in life, if we take time to reflect and learn from the knock, we will come back stronger, not weaker. The trick is to learn from the event presented to you, thus building your resilience in each situation. In a nutshell, resilience is the ability to manage high pressure and change and bounce back from adversity, thus reducing the adverse effects of stress that we experience during challenging times of change.

Imagine we have a cake called resilience, which we can slice into several pieces. Apart from coping strategies that can be healthy and unhealthy, many elements would make up the "Resilience Cake", including essentials such as mindset, purpose and a supportive community.

I was in a fortunate position, having done all the work on my inner self to have a mindset that helped me believe in myself and gave me confidence to handle the new storm. I was clear about my purpose, which gave me a reason for being each day and energised me. Most of all, I had an incredibly supportive community that provided me with many opportunities to share, be heard and be "held" during this rough patch of my life.

By now, having navigated my way through the 3D storms of life, I felt strong and competent. People asked me how I did it. How did I turn up each day with such a happy disposition and an optimistic outlook when I had just been dealt these rough life cards?

Well, I knew what I stood for, who I was and how I loved myself. I accepted the change and embraced the future with open arms. I was not afraid of what might happen anymore. I knew that I could—and had—survived many storms.

In some strange way, this storm of losing Dad so suddenly was the one when I learned to sail my boat of life properly. There is a beautiful saying: "A calm sea never made a skilled sailor." I was so grateful for all the previous storms that I had faced, as I felt skilled enough to navigate through this loss. I applied all the strategies I had in my navigation toolbox.

Turning to you, how do you navigate your storms?

Follow the steps I have proposed in previous chapters. By knowing yourself and being aware of areas of self-growth, you will find the magic that is missing so that you can shine brightly.

- Work on your inner self.

- Build your resilience.

- Let go and accept.

- Find out what drives you in life.

- Learn what is important to you.

- Find your purpose.

- Discover and re-evaluate your values along the way, for they, too, will change as your life evolves.

- Appreciate what you have.

- Be grateful for being you.

- Accept yourself for who you are.

Storms come and go. Learning to accept change is a massive part of life and that with each change or storm comes the gift of growth—should you choose—that will build your resilience each time. Learning to swim with the tide and stay afloat while building coping mechanisms will also help.

Remember, resilience is not a trait you have or do not have. It involves behaviours, thoughts and actions that anyone can learn and develop. The choice is yours. You can continue along your life path and blow in the wind like tumbleweed as life's storms happen, or you can anchor yourself by knowing yourself so that you may direct your way forward through each storm.

Each storm offers you another opportunity to choose your next path, to make another choice. Your power is within you now.

Storytime
The other side

One day, a young Buddhist came to the banks of a wide river on his journey home. Staring hopelessly at the significant obstacle before him, he pondered how to cross such a wide barrier for hours.

Just as he was about to give up his pursuit to continue his journey, he saw a great teacher on the other side of the river. The young Buddhist yelled to the teacher, "Oh, wise one, can you tell me how to get to the other side of this river?"

The teacher pondered momentarily, looked up and down the river, and yelled back, "My son, you are on the other side."

Exercise
Gratitude

Gratitude is yet another way of building strength within yourself. It helps you focus on the good and not the bad. Focus on feeding the wolf that brings light and hope. To do this, practice gratitude regularly and you will enhance your ability to be resilient and improve your wellbeing.

- Start a gratitude journal;

- Write down three to five things each day that you are grateful for;

- Keep this going for a week or preferably for a month;

- Notice how you feel about your day;

- Tell people you see every day what you appreciate about them.

Throughout this book, we have travelled through my storms of life, and I have provided you with ideas to pause, reflect and evaluate your inner self so that you may discover new ways to find more joy in your life.

Let's now look at how to find flow to make navigating your storm easier or any future storms you face.

Reflections

A space to capture your thoughts and ideas

INGRID FEAR

Chapter 7

Finding your flow

"Flow in the living moment. We are always in the process of becoming, and nothing is fixed."

- Bruce Lee

What is flow?

How do you find flow?

I get asked these questions by many people as I talk about flow.

Staying with the river analogy, we need to be like a river to flow and be open to new things in life, open to change and accepting that life will keep moving forward. It becomes our choice to find a way to work with our current state of life.

If we imagine that life is a river that flows at different paces and curves and carves out new courses as it moves through the various terrains, each of us is like a piece of driftwood bobbing along the river of life. As a piece of driftwood, to flow in the river, we need to avoid getting stuck against a big rock or in shallow waters where the flow is not strong enough to keep us moving forward. So, we need to let go of what has happened, relax in the river's flow and be prepared to keep moving forward with a clear focus on our ultimate destination. In this case, the destination could be self-confidence and joy.

What is flow and why do I keep talking about it?

The easiest way to describe flow is to get you to think about how you feel when you are involved in an activity you enjoy, so much that you lose all sense of time and awareness of everything else. Your focus is one hundred percent on the activity at hand. You are "in the moment", as Mihaly Csikszentmihalyi quotes in his book 'Flow'.

This activity could be playing a musical instrument, participating in a sport, painting a picture or writing a report. Flow is easily found in activities that require you to be creative. The state of flow is when you become so absorbed in an activity that it seems time has stood still. You are in the moment and become fully immersed in what you are doing.

Often, the activity you are engaged with strikes a delicate balance between the challenge of the task at hand and your skill level to achieve it, thus requiring intense focus and deep concentration as you immerse yourself in learning something new.

Finding your flow in life is important because this is where you grow, develop yourself and build your confidence. You will be in a state of flow if you know your purpose, have clarity about your direction and are aligned with your purpose and values. This will enable you to flow with the river of life. You will also notice that you will have a good sense of well-being.

Imagine living your life where everything is easy. Yet, you continue to grow and get lost in your sense of time and awareness of everything else. That sounds brilliant to me!

It sounds a lot better than living a life of struggle, unhappiness, boredom and obstacles.

We only get one chance at this life, so why not make some choices to live the rest of your life happy and in flow?

Reflecting on why I love paddleboarding and yoga, I realise that both are activities where I find the balance between challenging and developing my skills. I still have a lot to learn in both activities. The first time I stepped, or knelt, onto a paddleboard, I felt utterly pleased that I was on the river amongst nature. It required all my focus and concentration as I listened to the guide about what I needed to do next.

I wobbled down the river as my legs stood rigid and frozen to the board, fearing I would fall into the water. I did not dare to look up at anything we might be passing for fear of losing focus on what I needed to do. I was unsure if I enjoyed the first few experiences, but something switched within me. I began to think that I could enjoy paddleboarding if I persevered.

When I went out independently for those first few practice paddles, I focused on learning to do this new skill correctly. I was "in the zone". I corrected myself in stance and tenseness as I learned to relax and be on the river. Just me, the board (and paddle) and the river. We were at one with each other. The skill no longer requires much effort or intense focus, and the level of enjoyment is increasing. Now, I get lost in time after many times out on the river. I am at one with nature. I flow down the river and am in the zone while on board. Hours pass before I realise I am hungry, and it is time to get home. This is being in flow.

This act of losing track of time and disconnecting from external distractions is the psychological state of flow. It contributes to building resilience, a tool we need to navigate our storms.

Developing higher levels of self-confidence, tapping into more positive emotions and generally feeling great about yourself cannot be wrong. The more often you can access your "flow zone" the easier it is to navigate your life towards a more balanced one, where you can focus on looking after yourself and your well-being. And it goes without saying that this will give you an energised, positive and purposeful feeling.

As I have been saying all along, it is about choice. There are two alternate zones to the flow zone that you may find yourself in. These zones will either lead you towards a level of anxiety or stress, leading you to burnout if you continue along this path. Or the flip side is pure boredom, possibly leading you towards a place of rust out—the opposite of burnout. Neither one of these zones is where you find your flow. In both alternate zones, you will likely experience some dissatisfaction with your life.

If you find yourself, at this moment in time, leaning towards burnout or rust out, let's get you back on track and help you find your flow, or at least moments of flow in your life that will contribute to building your resilience and living a life of more joy.

I am not suggesting that there is no stress involved when you are in flow. You may experience good stress in the flow zone, also known as eustress. This is the stress you might feel before a first date or significant event. We feel a tingle of excitement, our bodies change, and we feel prepared, energised and ready to perform at our best.

How do you find flow in your life?

Think about what you enjoy doing or what you would like to achieve. Find something clear and specific to focus on. Maybe it will be a bit of a stretch for you, but it will be something that you would enjoy learning or doing and will be a manageable stretch that you give up soon. For me, this has been many things: walking the highest mountain in Africa, learning to paddleboard, learning yoga and learning the art of coaching.

Find someone who can provide feedback to keep growing and developing this area of your life. Something else to consider is stepping into this new learning environment where you can eliminate all external distractions.

For me, writing this book required me to get into flow. I chose to carve out regular time in my diary and created a garden space to reduce external distractions. All notifications were turned off, enabling me to focus on developing the creative skill of writing this book. As I write, I can hear the birds in the trees around me right now. I am in the flow zone.

Sometimes, it might take some time to quieten your mind so you can focus on the task in hand. This is where both meditation and mindfulness come into play. Both are helpful for getting you into a state of flow as they help quieten the mind and reduce the noise of external distractions. To meditate, you need to concentrate and filter out any distractions. Meditation will sharpen your mind to do precisely this!

Whether you are seeking to find the state of flow or simply looking after your mental well-being, learning the art of meditation or mindfulness will never hurt you. It can only contribute to navigating any life storm. Both will reduce anxiety and stress, giving you clarity of mind and space to consider your next life move.

Sustaining your state of flow plays a large part in handling and coping with any future challenges and stressors that might come your way. So, finding flow is not enough; you will need to find ways to sustain flow in your life to help navigate your future storms.

How can you sustain being in flow, you ask? We want to avoid that rust out state of boredom by keeping ourselves interested in life, new activities, new environments, continuing learning and staying engaged. You only have to ask any healthy octogenarian or centenarian what they recommend getting to their age and being "like them". They will all tell you to keep interested, keep engaging, be curious and continue to learn. And move!

I have a 91-year-old neighbour who still helms his boat up and down the River Thames as he takes his 60-year-old son and grandchildren to lunch further up the river. Each morning, when we bump into each other walking our dogs along the river, he has a range of questions about our lives and families.

Curiosity. Community. Commitment. Engagement.

He is learning new skills and living a life of flow where he is happy, learning, stretching, engaging, finding balance and is in a general state of well-being.

"If I was any better, I would be twins!" are the words of someone I had the privilege of working with many years ago. No matter what was going on in his life, he chose to step into each day with energy, optimism and curiosity for the day ahead.

My colleague never saw the negative side of life. If people around him pointed out the doom and gloom, he would quickly point out the good. His energy was infectious and attractive. People wanted to be around him.

He would share the story of two people who can go to the same event, one with a positive attitude and the other with a "mood hoover" attitude. The person with the positive attitude will walk away from the party having met interesting people, new contacts and having had a great evening. The "mood hoover" person is likely to have had a boring evening and not met anyone of interest. Same party, two different attitudes.

Choose your attitude. Do something you love. Vary your activities, learn new things, challenge yourself and make mistakes so that you learn, celebrate your achievements and find new communities of people. Try out new activities. You should only judge a new activity if you have tried it.

I judged yoga before I tried it. I thought it was not for me because I did not look like those who did it. After all, what would it do for me? I was sporty and loved challenging sports. It was not easy in the beginning, and what is more, I was surrounded by people the same age as my children, who all looked amazing in their fantastic yoga outfits. At the same time, I had the "muffin tops" spilling out over the top of my leggings while I tried hard not to look too awkward as I did my version of wrapping myself around myself, attempting to get into the various positions. And then, after perseverance and focus, I began to enjoy it.

I started to enjoy the calm. I noticed I could touch my toes without straining too many hamstring muscles. I began to appreciate the people around me. In time, I learned the deeper meaning of yoga when I found myself in floods of tears after a particular hip-opening session. Yoga is not just about stretching muscles. There is so much more to it than you see on the surface. It is now where I find my spiritual top-up in the week, alongside time in nature.

The more I persisted with learning yoga and getting into the zone in each session, the more I noticed that I was becoming physically stronger and, more importantly, less stressed. My mind was getting an opportunity to rest more often. I would find myself in flow in yoga. All that was required of me was to follow the instructions and connect with the moment. Through the many new breathing techniques I was learning, I found myself calmer and able to handle moments of stress more easily as I breathed into those moments.

I have found many areas of my life where I can access the flow zone. I have found my flow zone in yoga and paddleboarding. Both are new skills that I learned later in life. I continue to develop in both activities. They provide me with peace, calm and a state of being, contributing to my well-being.

Other areas where I find flow are within my work, where I coach and help develop people personally and professionally. My daily walks with the dog and gardening are other areas where I find flow and can connect with nature. This was starting to feel exactly right. I was finding balance and wanted to help even more people have this experience.

Even better is that these activities also align with my values of well-being and health. Hence, there is no resistance to taking myself off to either paddleboarding or yoga. I go with enthusiasm and keenness, whereas I notice with other activities where I have become bored or no longer getting what I want out of the activities, I find myself finding excuses not to go. For example, I enjoy a variety of outdoor circuit training.

When the cold, wet weather closed in, however, enjoying being outdoors during training became more challenging and I retreated to my couch. It became more difficult to motivate myself to go to the activity. During the colder months, training is brought inside or under a large roof to protect us from the wet weather. For me, this felt like I was no longer outdoors and was not quite what I enjoyed during the warmer months. For now, I have popped these activities into the "F*** it Bucket" until I am ready to bring them back into my life again, if I do.

We have spoken a lot about flow, and I would like to add additional supporting acts to help you navigate your storm. I have talked about mindset, thought patterns, choice, letting go of what no longer serves you and creating space for new things to come into your life.

Navigating your storm requires a mindset of self-belief and self-confidence while remaining true to your values and purpose. Finding a healthy balance and regularly looking after your well-being would help keep you motivated and energised. All of this will lead to a life of joy.

Self-confidence requires kindness toward yourself, continuing to learn and develop and standing up for yourself. To believe in yourself, you need to know what you stand for.

Who are you now?

What do you want now?

How do you discover who you are and what you stand for? Two little words are very important and often get ignored in life: purpose and values.

Before moving on, finding flow is about learning a new skill and immersing yourself in the learning while being connected to the moment where you lose all sense of time and external distractions. It is where you build your resilience and confidence as you expand your comfort zone and community. It also requires a high level of quietness in your mind so that you can focus. Meditation and mindfulness are great tools to help you get into your flow zone.

Storytime
The belief of the elephant

For those of you who know my work, I often share elephant stories to convey a message. I would love to share this parable with you to help you realise that sometimes we need to challenge what we believe to be true to achieve our flow.

This story is about a person who is curious how an adult elephant that weighs between four and six tonnes is held in one place by a simple rope around its ankle and a steel stake approximately two meters high. Surely, the elephant is stronger than the rope and stake and simply needs to nudge the stake out of the ground and move away?

The elephant does not take this action because the rope and stake were attached to its ankle when it was a baby elephant. At that time, the rope and stake were more robust. Any attempts that the baby elephant may have taken to pull away from the stake would have been in vain. Thus, the elephant grew up with a conditional belief that every time the rope was tied around its ankle and attached to the stake in the ground, it would not have the strength or power to move away, resulting in a life of being stuck to its environment and a sense of being controlled.

Challenge your beliefs as they may be holding you back from finding a life of flow.

Exercise
Finding your flow state

I am going to leave this exercise for you each to discover yourselves. Go for the stretch and begin to learn something new and challenging where you can get lost in time.

Find your flow state so that you can continue to evolve and grow. I would love for you to learn this skill so that you can live your life flowingly. You move through life with ease, confidence and clarity. You are strong and resilient. You have joy in your life. You delete the external noise of what others might think. You are excited about your future path. You have more fun. You believe in yourself.

Help yourself find your own flow by discovering a new skill. Find something to learn that might be challenging at first but enjoyable for you, where you might meet new people, find a new tribe and grow your confidence in yourself.

Remember the ferryman's advice: Get clear on what you want to achieve, give yourself time to learn and do not judge; only observe and notice what you can do better next time.

The more you can access your flow zone, the easier it will be to navigate all your future storms of life. Invest in yourself now so that you wobble less when the storm hits.

Grab a nature snack from time to time.

Create boundaries.

Learn to say no to what does not serve you.

Say yes to the new.

Connect with your purpose.

Love and respect yourself, always.

Reflections

A space to capture your thoughts and ideas

Chapter 8

Finding the real you

"Knowing others is wisdom; knowing yourself is enlightenment."

- Lao Tzu

How do you establish who you are now? Life revolves around us. There is constant change, and we need to work with the change. Life happens to us. Perhaps you are at yet another crossroads of life and find yourself at yet another choice point in time.

You have learned the power of pause and self-reflection. You have learned to explore more about your belief systems and understand what it might be like to be in the flow of life. This chapter will dig deeper to help you find the real you.

There are many levels of self-discovery. In this chapter, we will tap into those two words that help us find ourselves and what we stand for, keep us on our path with confidence in who we are and help us quickly make decisions. The first is "purpose" and the second is "values".

As part of my self-growth and development of self-belief while creating a life of joy, these are two elements that I focused on a lot and continue to revisit as I evolve and adapt what I do in life to live my best life and navigate all storms that come my way.

It would be my absolute pleasure to guide you down this path so that you, too, can find joy and continue to flow with life.

Purpose and values are two compelling words with a lot of punch and deep meaning and should be addressed when seeking to find the real you.

Purpose is about having meaning in life and knowing why you do what you do.

Personal values are the pillars on which you build your life. They are how you live your life.

The word "purpose" comes into my life almost every day. Finding purpose in each of my days is what keeps me moving forward. A day without meaning is a day wasted for me. Connecting (most) of my daily activities to my purpose keeps me in flow.

A great example of a non-purposeful day is often experienced in working environments, where people turn up to receive their monthly salary yet are disengaged with colleagues and the business itself.

Working without a purpose or being able to connect the dots to the bigger picture is unhelpful in finding flow. It would also certainly drain your energy, depleting your natural resources and passion and working against your well-being, making it more challenging to navigate a storm when it next arises. It takes a lot more out of us to handle storms in our lives if we start from a place of depleted energy.

Purpose is not something that you will necessarily discover overnight.

Everyone has a purpose in this world. We might not all be Mahatma Gandhi, Nelson Mandela, Mother Theresa or Martin Luther King; we have our world, and having a sense of purpose will bring us daily joy. Your purpose can be as simple as "to live a life of health", "to be happy" or "to be kind". Holding onto these purpose statements daily gives you a sense of direction and a feeling of connectedness. You can consider whether you lived your purpose at the end of each day. Was I kind to myself today? Was I kind to my family, work colleagues, strangers, or the world in general?

How much joy would this reflection bring you, knowing that your day had been purposeful and fulfilling? It's much better than saying at the end of the day, "What's the point? Life is boring. I have nothing to do. There is nothing new and exciting."

With this attitude or language, you will have less joy and probably mood hoover yourself into lowered confidence and less joy in your world.

Finding your values and purpose is part of a more extensive exercise that may require you to work with a coach. However, let us begin.

Let's start with your values. Knowing your values will help you make decisions far easier in life, particularly when facing one of life's storms.

We all have values that we adhere to when making decisions in our lives.

Some of you will already be aware of your values; others won't because our values build up through our life experiences in a process, we are only sometimes aware of. One of the most frequently observed psychological phenomena is "cognitive dissonance" where a person holds two conflicting beliefs simultaneously because they are not adequately aware of each. The area between the two contradictory ideas and behaviour will cause mental discomfort in the person. An example of cognitive dissonance is that you want to be healthy. Yet, you do not exercise regularly or eat nutritious food. As a result, you feel guilty and will notice them all the time.

Many of us hold similar values in life. But because life has changed, the values we need or use to guide our lives today may differ from those we needed or used to guide our lives ten years ago.

Imagine that we all have a book that is entitled with our name. Our name is printed on the front cover and this book is one-hundred pages long. Each one of the one-hundred pages has one of your values printed on it, resulting in a book listing your top one hundred values. The first five pages list your current priority values.

Generally, we operate our lives with between five and seven values at any time. For example, when I was younger and in my early twenties, I would have based many of my life decisions on finance, wealth, health, career, family, and happiness. Today, after the road I have travelled and you have now shared, the values that drive my decisions are family; independence; wellness; adventure; and trust.

So, to go back to the little book of values that we each have. The first page of my book will have the word "family" printed on it. Page two will be "independence".

Page three will be "wellness". Page four is "adventure". And page five is "trust".

Even though you and I may share similar values, they might mean different things to each of us. For example, this is what these five values mean to me.

Family: Time with blood and extended family members is not negotiable.

Independence: Confidence in myself to navigate my life the way I choose.

Wellness: Mental, physical, emotional and spiritual health, happiness whilst being fuelled by nature.

Adventure: Growing and learning through new challenges.

Trust: People around me are reliable, consistent, open, and speak truthfully.

These five words are how I make my life decisions. Notice that the value words finance, career and wealth are not in my top five today because my life has evolved. I have come to realise that true wealth in life is not about financial wealth but rather about health and happiness.

The experience I shared with you at the beginning of this book, which resulted in debt and, ultimately, divorce, increased my value of independence. To be able to navigate future storms, I needed to make different decisions, operating from different guiding principles or values.

Your values are personal to you, and they give you your sense of identity. They are at the heart of your judgment and way of life. With values, we can maintain our sense of who we are.

Values are complicated and are not as simple as saying, "Live by your values." Values will have both a positive and a negative side to them. There are no absolute "good" values. We might say, for example, generosity is a perceived positive value, and I don't just mean material generosity. I am talking about someone willing to listen to others and find themselves being the giver in most relationships. This may lead to the feeling that you are undervalued and even a sense of being used.

The act of giving is admirable. On the flip side, receiving can require tremendous generosity of spirit and, ultimately, may even be more generous. Giving can be controlling or even manipulative. Yet, allowing someone the opportunity to give can be very selfless and gracious. Understanding this paradox will help you appreciate your actions. It may also help when you feel undervalued as a "selfless" giver in a relationship!

Likewise, independence is a core value for me. It often gets me into trouble by not wanting to be restrained by anyone or anything. I have my views and given my life choices. I prefer not to depend on anyone. I have learned to work more with interdependence. Of course, should there be a life-altering event, it may require that I have no choice in the matter and be dependent upon another. This would be outside of my control.

We are talking about making choices and choosing values that support your ability to be in control of your life. We cannot control the world's politics and what others say or do with their lives. However, we can control our actions, behaviours and thoughts.

For me, it is essential that I "drive my bus of life" forward. The thoughts I have around this value will drive my emotions and actions and are all (mostly) within my control.

Here is the beautiful thing about knowing what you stand for. Knowing my values enables me to make choices in life that give me a feeling of independence. I mostly avoid situations where my independence is compromised so that I feel good about myself. However, this high driver for independence can impact relationships and opportunities, as others may deem me selfish and uncaring. Accepting and learning to be interdependent has been my saviour. This awareness came to light after doing some self-reflection.

Our values are generally established by the time we are adults. Still, life experiences and contact with others can cause them to change. As mentioned earlier, regular self-reflection on your values to sense whether they still serve you or are still important at this time in your life is a helpful exercise.

You can access your values right now, but this may be a stretch if you have yet to self-reflect. In the exercise below, I will provide a little cheat's way of eliciting your values. This exercise may be something that you wish to speak with a coach about, as it can sometimes trigger all sorts of emotions within.

Finding out who you really are and what you stand for can be quite an eye-opener, particularly if you have lost your way along the path of life by being in the river of life and going where it takes you.

A tip to give you an indication of your values is to begin analysing things that don't seem to be going right. Notice where you judge someone's behaviour and actions. Or perhaps something does not feel right. Find time to reflect upon what might be driving this feeling or observation. Often, your values will come to light through this self-reflection.

Living your life true to your values will also require courage and strength to create boundaries around you as you learn to say "no" to things that no longer support you or fill up your cup. You do not wish to be drained in life.

It can be challenging to create these boundaries and very confusing for people around you if they are directly impacted. Remember, you are here to find the tools and skills to navigate your storm. The best way to navigate your storm is by putting your oxygen mask on first. Look after yourself first and then you can care for others too. Boundaries are a kind of oxygen mask.

What boundaries do you need to create?

The Covid-19 pandemic—while a shock to the system to have such radical changes thrown into our lives—in hindsight, the "pause of life", as it was, highlighted to many what is important to them and what they were no longer prepared to do.

Many companies struggled and continue to struggle to get people to commute long distances to go back into the office. Primarily, the reasons for getting people back into the office were with positive intent: people have worked out what a drain on their personal lives commuting was. People have discovered how much more they can do with their lives with the additional commute time being given back to their families and personal lives.

For me, this amounted to an average of three hours commute per day. Fifteen hours per week is nearly an additional two working days per week, which slowly eroded over time as we learned to believe that money is important. And to earn this money, we needed to work in the city. It became socially acceptable that if you worked in the City of London, you must have a good job. And I am sure this is true of all other cities worldwide, too. No wonder people were exhausted and limped their way to retirement when, only then, could they have a life of joy.

I am thankful to the pandemic for raising awareness, at least, about what boundaries I wanted to create around me to enjoy life even more. Thank you, too, for allowing me space to reflect and recharge. The pandemic was yet another choice point for me, as it was for many others.

At the time that the pandemic struck, while I was loving the work I was doing, I noticed that I was giving more and more of myself to work. While my pre-Covid work aligned with my purpose of "living my best life while inspiring others to live their best lives" by delivering coaching and workshops to help people grow and develop, I was beginning to burn out. I was tired and no longer enjoying my work. I was starting to think that something needed to change. "Be careful what you wish for!"

We were granted months of reflection time during the pandemic. This was a challenging time for some, but as the saying goes, "We are not all in the same boat. We might be in the same storm but are all in different boats. Some have oars and some have no oars." The storm of the pandemic was a big one for each of us to navigate. Getting through that storm was tough as there were things inside our control and many outside our control.

This was a time to connect with myself, understand who I was, and consider what was now important to me. More importantly, it raised awareness of choosing to whom and what I listened to while filtering through sensationalism, truth, reality and deception. I also chose how much of the news to focus on and on what I could control: my mental state and well-being.

So, I began to create healthy boundaries, such as "deleting" specific media channels from my life (again) and instead tuning into optimism and what could be done, not what was forbidden.

These healthy boundaries included not getting drawn into the daily updates on the pandemic numbers and instead continuing with daily exercise. My partner and I focused on our well-being and health. We walked more! We walked along the river to buy our vegetables from the open-air market as we had more time granted to us. We gardened more. We planted our vegetables and exchanged products with neighbours and friends. We walked to friends' houses to drop off gifts to keep our spirits high. We communicated more. A large community was formed where people found time to talk and enquire about each other. We embraced Zoom and spoke with family members we had lost connection with. We all had the gift of time. One of the highest commodities in life is time.

How many of you are still walking, or have you slipped back into the demands and expectations of life?

The pandemic is when Captain, our dog, entered our lives. We rescued him from living in restricted conditions so we could walk even more! We walked amongst nature. We had joy in our lives. We met new people. We met our neighbours and had real meaningful conversations with them and continue to do so. Who would have thought you could meet new people during a "lockdown"? Mindset! Choice! Values!

The lockdown caused a great divide among family, friends and neighbours as people tapped into different mindsets and operated from other values and belief systems. And so, as you continue to "find you" through reflection, personal values, mindset and creating boundaries, the second word that I promised we would visit remains: purpose.

How does finding purpose contribute to finding you? Quite simply, your purpose will keep you on track in life. It will provide the fuel to propel your boat forward in your storm. When you have meaning in your life, it is effortless to flow.

You may have come across the term "Ikigai" (pronounced ick-ee-guy), a Japanese concept that means "your reason for being" or "your life purpose". Japanese life expectancy is one of the highest in the world. While their diet contributes a lot to increased life expectancy, there is also a belief that "ikigai" plays a large part in their longevity.

By knowing your "ikigai", or purpose, you naturally connect with people of the same ilk. You build strong communities around your interests, motivating you to be with these people. You have a sense of achievement as you go about your days doing what you love. You live a life of enjoyment and joy, all contributing to a healthy mindset and general well-being. You are energised.

Would you like me to help you find your purpose in life?

As I mentioned earlier, finding your purpose is sometimes something that happens over time. It begins by finding time to reflect and asking yourself some rather deep and meaningful questions that might be hard to answer initially. Finding your purpose will require patience, a lot of self-reflection and listening to others as you find your passions.

I cannot tell you how many people I have coached who come to me unhappy in life or work. They want to climb the ranks of the corporate ladder because that is what others expect of them. That is where they can earn more money and gain recognition. Perhaps another title will make them feel better! And when we get to the nuts and bolts of the coaching process, it is often about happiness and finding joy.

Happiness and joy come with having a good sense of purpose and a healthy dose of well-being. Having a title, a large pot of money or a big house does not necessarily equip us with the fuel to weather life's storms.

To help you find your purpose, I propose opening your journal. If you've not yet started, now is the time to begin journaling. Perhaps your journal, similar to the proposed "Personal Value Book" has one question per page. Perhaps your journal, similar to the proposed "Personal Value Book" has one question per page. For example:

- What do I love doing?

- What do people ask me to help them with?

- What do I think the world needs more of?

- What might you regret never doing, achieving, or experiencing?

Each time you find time to reflect, ponder on the above questions, and notice how your responses align or vary over time.

A little clue when searching for your purpose is that it will often be about helping another person or persons. Having a purpose is not selfish, it is about being and doing good for another, the wider community or the world itself.

It is also worth noting that finding your purpose may take years as you continue to explore life. Remember, it does not have to be something significant; it can be as simple as wanting to help people by volunteering. Finding purpose does not necessarily mean you will be changing your work. It might be that you are already doing the thing you love, and you only want a little tweak to refuel yourself.

So, back to the journalling and reflective questions: you may ask questions of yourself as you seek out your purpose or Ikigai.

Start by thinking about what you love doing. This could be at work, or perhaps it is a hobby you have. For me, it was my love of teaching and helping people grow. Hence, coaching and developing people personally and professionally.

Next, explore what you are good at. The way to discover this is to think about what advice people seek from you. What do people ask you to help them with? Is it something at work, or perhaps it is something in your personal life? Again, I noted that people always asked me to sound them out, bounce things off them, or, in other words, listen. Listening is a massive element of coaching.

And the next part is where it can feel overwhelming. I encourage you to think carefully, go with what comes to mind and write it down. What do you think the world needs? It could be kindness, or even another app. Steve Jobs said the world needed people who are empowered. He wanted to make a dent in the universe. Also, consider what you might regret not doing, being or having.

And, of course, a very tough part of a finding purpose exercise is casting your mind forward to a time when you will be ninety years old. Imagine yourself sitting on a rocking chair in your garden or on your balcony, and you are content with the life you have lived, all that you have achieved and all the people you have met along the way. As you reflect upon your life, you ponder what has mattered to you most. Make a note of these in your journal.

The above questions and scenarios will begin to lead you towards discovering your purpose. Please find time to reflect on your answers and find a way to summarise your collective thoughts into a short statement or short sentence, making it easy for you to access.

My example is: "Living my best life while inspiring others to live their best."

You will know you have found your purpose because you feel joyful and fully connected to the world. You feel as though you have a home and belong. You are no longer seeking; instead, you begin to live a life of flow as you turn up each day to do what you do best and live your purpose.

This is when you have truly found yourself.

Finding the real you will require time to reflect and consider your highlights and low lights in life thus far. Consider what you stand for by eliciting your values that help you make your daily decisions. Visit your values will help you surface the non-negotiables in your life and where you are prepared to compromise. Create healthy boundaries around yourself to manage being you is important.

Suppose you already know exactly who you are. In that case, it may be that you are not living according to what is important to you because your boundaries are not in place. You are operating on older values that are no longer as important at this time in your life. This is an indication to reevaluate.

Storytime
The three bricklayers

The story of three bricklayers has many variations yet hails from the great fire in London during 1666. Christopher Wren, the famous architect at the time, was engaged to rebuild St Paul's Cathedral which had been destroyed during the fire.

He observed three bricklayers on a scaffolding, one was crouched, one was half-standing and the third stood tall, working very hard and fast.

Christopher Wren approached the three bricklayers and asked each of them the question, "What are you doing?"

The first bricklayer responded, "I'm a bricklayer. I'm working hard laying bricks to feed my family."

The second bricklayer, responded, "I'm a builder. I'm building a wall."

And, the third bricklayer, responded with a gleam in his eye, "I'm a cathedral builder. I'm building a great cathedral."

The third bricklayer had a purpose. He was connected to the reason for his job leaving him with high motivation and a positive attitude.

Exercise
Finding the real you through identifying your top 5 values.

Again, it would be best if you took some time out of your day to do this exercise. This can be a deeply reflective exercise, so ensure you give yourself space and recognise that you are about to head down memory lane for a good reason. You are about to work towards finding the real you through your current top five values.

Step One: Find a quiet space with pen and paper and centre yourself.

Step Two: Review the short list of values below.

This list is not infinite, so if you feel there are value words you hold dear that are not on this list, please add them. Then, follow the instructions and trust your gut.

Authenticity	Challenge	Faith	Independence
Achievement	Citizenship	Fame	Influence
Adventure	Community	Family	Justice
Authority	Competency	Friendships	Kindness
Autonomy	Contribution	Fun	Knowledge
Balance	Creativity	Growth	Leadership
Beauty	Curiosity	Happiness	Learning
Boldness	Determination	Honesty	Love
Compassion	Fairness	Humour	Loyalty

Meaningful Work	Popular	Self-Respect	Unique
Openness	Recognition	Service	Wealth
Optimism	Religion	Spirituality	Wellbeing
Peace	Reputation	Stability	Wisdom
Perfection	Respect	Status	Zealous
Pleasure	Responsibility	Success	
	Security	Trustworthiness	

Step Three: Filter and rank.

- Circle any "value" words that you are drawn towards.

- Review the circled words and write them in a separate list.

- Decide if any values circled are no longer important to you now.

- Rank the remaining values in order of importance to you. To do this, ask yourself, "Which of these is most important to me?" Continue until you have a list of five "value" words, your top five for today!

Step Four: Find the backstory.

Each identified value will have a "backstory" attached to them. As you know, values will come from your lived experiences. The identified values may all be closely connected in meaning and origin. This step will take time as you reflect on various events in your life where these values may have been instilled.

The stories may be moments of fantastic enjoyment where the family got together, laughed and connected a lot. Or they may be moments of sadness, loss, pride, love or pure joy. Do not judge these moments; they are part of your life and have formed you to be exactly who you are today. From these backstories, you have carved out your guidelines for living your life today.

Enjoy this process as you head down memory lane.

These words will help you discover who you are and realise why you desire or behave in a certain way. Be proud of who you are, I am.

Step Five: Write these five "value" words down.

Place these written down words where you can see them daily as a reminder of your guidelines in life. Maybe you would like to draw a picture that aligns with the associated backstory to each of the five value words. Capturing memories in images is sometimes easier to access the memory than reading a word. This will help remind you of exactly who you are and where your values were instilled.

Well done! Enjoy and good luck! Now breathe...

Reflections

A space to capture your thoughts and ideas

Chapter 9

Flow with Ease

"Self-care is not selfish.
You cannot serve from an empty vessel."
- Eleanor Brown

Going back to earlier in this book, I referenced not wanting to be like a piece of driftwood bobbing along in the flow of a river and going where it directed me. This would mean that I would need to go where the river took me and move at the pace of the flow at the time. It would also mean occasionally getting caught or stuck in troubled or still waters where I would feel out of my depth or perhaps not connected and "at one" with life. I have come to realise that it only takes a little nudge or a shift of thought to get myself back in the gentle flow of the river of life.

This nudge can be self-driven, or at times, it may require a little support from another person, a coach, or a friend who has your best interests at heart. Someone willing to be your best friend by balancing the relationship. Someone contributing to your confidence, self-belief and joy in life.

Whatever storm you face in the future—because you will—you want to be in the best place to navigate your way through your future storm and easily flow in the river of life. The way to do this is to ensure you are prepared. Many of the exercises outlined in the previous chapters of this book will form part of your preparation to navigate through future life storms.

Let's imagine that you are no longer that piece of driftwood being directed by the river. Instead, you have chosen to take back an element of control by flowing in the river of life in a raft. This raft has you at the helm and you get to choose the speed and destination of your journey every day.

You navigate confidently and excitedly about what might be around the next corner. Your raft is well prepared to handle all eventualities, and it can adapt to the environment. It can take on board additional crew to strengthen your power to steer through stormy and murky waters. You may need to reach out to people on the banks for help to clear the deadwood or obstacles that get in your way of flowing easily. Choose these people wisely.

You get to choose to enjoy the scenery along the way and accept that the pace of the current will change as the river either meanders along the floodplain or carves a new course through narrow rock.

This raft comprises all the elements you need to feel supported and loved. It will take care of you no matter what the conditions. You are clear about what is important to you and will not take on board crew who seek to drain your energy or take you off course. Your life raft is kitted with resilience, reframing and breathing techniques, self-belief, confidence and joy. Your inner strength is driven by your self-belief, and you are guided by your core values as you flow through the river of life.

Having visualised your growth and strength in life's journey, you are confident that you will reach your chosen destination whole and not drained. At all times, you feel whole, connected, confident and at ease with yourself to navigate through the storm at hand. Stay focused on your end goal and prepare for detours, for they will build your resilience.

You choose to take time to refuel and take care of yourself along the way. Refuel your energy by remaining true to yourself, taking care of your well-being, and connecting with the reason for your journey. Be self-aware and recognise the times when it is important to be still, reflect and restore

Throughout this book, we have discussed many tools and techniques that you can use to help build your confidence and find joy in your life again. I hope you have tried out a few of the exercises shared with you and are feeling inspired so that you can reset and begin to flow again.

You will have noted how important it is to approach all challenges with the right mindset. Developing yourself through constant personal growth will contribute to your feeling confident about yourself. Steering your raft through the river of life will require an open, optimistic and resilient mindset.

Everything I have shared with you in this book can be summarised in what I call my MBA: a simple approach to doing a daily check-in on yourself.

MBA stands for Mindset, Balance, and Action.

Daily, I give myself a little check-in to graduate with an MBA. For someone who has gone through the University of Life, this is quite a powerful way of building my confidence and self-belief.

Imagine the imposter syndrome I had when I entered the corporate environment, where people began by introducing themselves with academic credentials to make them feel confident and powerful. All I wanted to know was, "Who are you?".

Your academic credentials are excellent, and I respect them. However, they do not make you a better person if you are unkind and seek to belittle or mood hoover others around you.

My invitation to everyone is to let people know who you are. People follow people, not titles. People follow those with good values and open belief systems. No one wants to be in the room with arrogance. The latter feeds into the "mood hoover" group of people.

I invite you to join me for a daily MBA graduation so that we feel confident in ourselves, recognise where we might be wavering in our self-belief and understand what is draining the joy from our lives.

Starting with the "M" of MBA. Mindset.

Getting your mindset in the right direction of being open to new things, growth, possibility, embracing challenges and having an optimistic view of the future will set you up to attract the right people into your life and more opportunities. Suppose you keep judging yourself and others or shutting yourself down and away from others. In that case, your world will become smaller and lonely, and you may be put into the mood hoover camp of another. Learn to be "your own best friend".

Next, the "B" of the MBA. Balance

To flow with ease requires that you remain in balance. By this, I mean taking care of yourself physically, mentally, spiritually and emotionally. Make sure that you are in a healthy state of well-being. Respecting yourself and acknowledging what you need to do to ensure that your energy is always topped up and that you feel fuelled, energised, motivated and have a happy disposition each day. Balance requires being kind to yourself and regular self-care. Being in balance will bring you joy each day as you have a sense of being in control when you are in balance. You can choose what can be cleared from your daily tasks or what you hold in your head. When out of balance, we feel resentment, anger and jealousy.

Finally, the "A" of MBA. Action

Creating the right mindset and finding a healthy balance requires daily action. Each day is an opportunity to shift your perspective and adjust the balance scale that you find yourself in. This comes back to the Law of Attraction touched upon earlier in this book. There is no value in simply visualising or imagining that there is a different "you" unless you act. Help yourself move forward towards being your optimal best.

Below is a set of questions you can ask yourself to ensure you graduate with a daily MBA.

Mindset: Give yourself a "check-up from the neck-up".

- Do I have kind and loving thoughts about myself today?

- Are my thoughts about the day ahead open?

- Am I feeling purposeful and motivated?

Balance: Check the weight of your scale.

- Am I tipping out of balance by having too much on my plate today?

- Is my energy able to sustain me for today's activities?

- Can I do something to help bring myself into balance for today?

Action: Choose an action you can take to graduate today.

- What affirmation will I use today to balance myself?

- Who or what will I connect with today to bring me joy and confidence?

- How will I be my best friend throughout today?

Knowing who you are and what you stand for helps you perform at your best. Being able to confidently be yourself and reduce the pain of indecisiveness gives you control. As we have said before, being clear about your values and purpose and living a life of balance will lead to a life of joy and flow.

So, take control of who you are and get back at the helm if you still need to do this. Be clear about your next steps. Know your chosen route. Find your tribe. Take care of yourself.

Here are some simple examples of how I live my life today to ensure that my confidence remains intact and that I end each day knowing it was joyful. You will have your own to draw upon. I only share these to highlight that we must keep life simple and not overcomplicated. Make time for the right things and people in your life. It is your choice.

I do my daily MBA check-in.

In addition, I tune into my emotions throughout the day and make sure that I am not over or underplaying them. Equally, if I notice that something has triggered me and I feel angry, I consider what part of me or my value system has been challenged.

I have learned to accept what is within my control.

I embrace nature daily by walking the dog, gardening or listening to the birds in the trees. Nature is my church. There is no judgment in nature. The birds sing and the trees listen, working in harmony. After each storm, there is regrowth.

I find time to move each day. Whether for a gentle walk along the river, a yoga class, or a more intense form of exercise such as playing tennis or pickleball with some friends. Movement is vital to feeling physically well. The more often we move within each day, the better it is for our overall well-being.

I want to leave you with some parting thoughts: Whatever your storm is, know that there will be more and understand that you can navigate through all your storms by reminding yourself that you are at the helm of your raft in the river of life. You control your thoughts, and you get to choose what you say "yes" or "no" to.

Finding joy is within your gift. Joy does not happen to us. It is about daily choice. Discovering what brings you joy and what does not is part of clearing the deadwood we discussed earlier. Make finding joy part of your daily MBA graduation.

Delete what no longer serves you.

Consider what you need to bring more of into your life.

Permit yourself to be joyful.

This joy will come from being confident in being you, believing in yourself, following your passions and being healthy. When we look at the element of well-being and resilience, joy is about being present in the now. Joy is an internal state that sits beneath a busy mind's surface. Allow joy to emerge by connecting with your emotions and feelings and quietening the mind. You can choose to experience joy right now if you wish. Be in the moment. Experience presence and discover joy in that moment. Desiring happiness or joy in the future is not appreciating what you have or who you are right now. Choose joy now. Joy is that inner feeling where you feel genuinely connected and purposeful. That is joy.

Please find time to refuel yourself and learn to accept what it is.

Live with kindness in your heart and mind.

Set healthy boundaries by confidently saying "no" to what no longer serves you.

Love and respect yourself always.

Live your best life purposefully by living your truth through your values.

Exercise
Live a daily life of FLOW

F - Find time to do your daily MBA check-in.

L - Love yourself by being kind in thought.

O - Overcome challenges by tapping into your resources.

W - Walk into your future with confidence, self-belief and joy.

Notice your growth in confidence and self-belief as you lean into navigating the river of life. Enjoy the sense of pride and joy as you emerge from each storm.

Live a life of flowing with ease.

Reflections

A space to capture your thoughts and ideas

INGRID FEAR

References

Frankl, Viktor. Man's Search for Meaning (CPI Cox & Wyman, Reading, 2004)

Csikszentmihalyi, Mihaly. Flow (Clays Ltd,Elcograf S.p.A, 2002)

McMichael, Gillian. Coming Home (Panoma Press Ltd, 2022)

Stone, Sue. Love life, live life (Hemmick Press, 2007)

Mayne, Brian. Goal Mapping (Watkins Publishing, London, 2007)

Byrne, Rhonda. The Secret DVD (TM TS Production LLC, 2006)

The King Story, Zenwave Studios, YouTube ZenWave Studios - YouTube

Aesops Fables

About the Author

Ingrid Fear is an experienced Leadership Development Facilitator, Wellness Coach and Speaker who thrives on supporting people to achieve their optimal confident self.

Born in South Africa, she now lives in the United Kingdom with a globally dispersed family. Ingrid is passionate about growth, nature and travel resulting in a curiosity to explore and experience new environments and adventures.

Ingrid has overcome many challenges in life and has chosen to live a life of balance by focusing on personal wellness in a world of constant pressure and change.

Ingrid has desired to write a book and share her story to inspire and encourage others to keep moving forward and believe in themselves while keeping a keen eye on having a life of balance no matter the situation.

To connect or work with Ingrid:

Visit www.ingridfear.co.uk

Follow on Instagram: Ingrid Fear (@optimalmindset_ingrid)

Follow on LinkedIn: Ingrid Fear - Optimal Mindset and Wellness Coach |

INGRID FEAR

About PublishU

PublishU enables you to tell your story or communicate your message by writing and publishing a book worldwide.

"I never thought I would be able to write a book, let alone in 100 days… now I'm asking what else have I told myself that I can't do that I actually can?'"

PublishU Author

To find out more visit

www.PublishU.com

Printed in Great Britain
by Amazon

57680252R00086